BR: From G
to Blue

RUSSELL SAXTON

Key Books

BRITAIN'S RAILWAYS SERIES, VOLUME 4

Opening images: Title page, Class 47 D1610 at Salisbury on 29 August 1964. Contents page, Class 22 D6343 at Royal Oak in June 1968. Foreword, Deltic D9006 at Darlington on 30 April 1968.

Published by Key Books
An imprint of Key Publishing Ltd
PO Box 100
Stamford
Lincs PE19 1XQ

www.keypublishing.com

The right of Russell Saxton to be identified as the author of this book has been asserted in accordance with the Copyright, Designs and Patents Act 1988 Sections 77 and 78.
Copyright © Russell Saxton, 2020

Acknowledgements
A special thank you to Ron Halestrap and Neil Phillips for nigh on two decades of selfless and untiring help and the fantastic generosity they constantly supplied.

ISBN 978 1 913295 91 2

All rights reserved. Reproduction in whole or in part in any form whatsoever or by any means is strictly prohibited without the prior permission of the Publisher.

Acronyms
GSYP – Green with Small Yellow Panels
BSYP – Blue with Small Yellow Panels
GFYE – Green with Full Yellow Ends
BFYE – Blue with Full Yellow Ends

Typeset by SJmagic DESIGN SERVICES, India.

Contents

Foreword	4
BR: From Green to Blue	5
Peaks	5
Class 40	9
Class 50	12
D600s	13
'Warships'	14
Class 52	17
Class 47	19
Class 03	24
Class 04	25
Class 06	26
Class 05	27
Class 01	28
Class 02	28
Unclass.	29
Class 07	30
Class 08/9/10/3	31
Class 24	37
Class 25	42
Class 26	46
Class 27	47
Class 31	51
Class 28	54
Class 23	54
Class 21	55
Class 29	56
Class 22	57
Class 33	59
Class 37	61
'Hymeks'	64
Class 20	68
Class 15	71
Class 16	72
Class 17	73
Class 55	74
Class 56	76
Class 53	76
Prototypes and Ex-big 4	77
Class 70	80
Class 73	80
Class 76	82
Class 77	84
Electrics 81-87	85
DMUs	88
EMUs	90

Foreword

One of the most fascinating eras for the lover of modern traction is the changeover from the old British Railways liveries to the corporate blue and grey of post-1965 British Rail. I was a small boy in the 1960s, already hooked on railways and born just too late to be able to remember steam as much more than a hazy childhood memory. Our earliest recollections are often the most formative and I was captivated by the changing railway scene of the mid to late 1960s up to the early 1970s, as the green and maroon liveries applied to locos and coaching stock disappeared to be replaced by the new Rail Blue for locos and the blue and grey for coaching stock.

Because rail enthusiasts were preparing to mourn the passing of the steam locomotive, comparatively little attention was focused on the modern scene. Many of the changes went almost unrecorded and unphotographed. Some of the most interesting motive power, which was unfortunate enough to be withdrawn whilst steam was fresh in the memory, went to the scrapyard, something that would be unthinkable in these days of preserving everything that moved.

In this book I have tried to give a general overview of the changes at this time and to list as many variations in livery style as possible. To cover everything photographically is both impractical and impossible because so much escaped the lens as photographers put away their cameras for a few years, but I hope that I have covered every major variation.

The older British Railways image lasted far longer than British Rail intended. I was yet to start school when Rail Blue appeared and yet I was working for a living before the last green-liveried locos disappeared in the very early 1980s. It was, for me and my generation of enthusiasts, a time of great interest and I hope you will enjoy this look back at our collective youth.

BR: From Green to Blue

Peaks

The classic lined out green-liveried 'Peak' is wonderfully illustrated by D92 at Holbeck in June 1966, a style worn by all 193 locos across the three classes. The long white stripe and the lined out grills break up the lengthy sides of the locos, whereas the economy examples had a less pleasing appearance, looking rather slab-sided. All the 44s, most of the 45s and the first few 46s were all delivered minus yellow panels. Class 45s D50-67 and maybe the last handful in the D108-37 series had them from new, as did the majority of Class 46s. The last 44 in green was D6 until September 1973, the last 45 was D119 until February 1970 and the last 46 was D165 until September 1972. (Charlie Cross, Gordon Edgar collection)

Above: Between 1965 and 1966 newly overhauled 'Peaks' lost the attractive lined green livery for a more basic style dubbed 'Economy Green'. Here is the newly overhauled D62 at Nottingham on 3 September 1966. Examples of all three variants appeared in this style, minus all lining but retaining the serif numbers and Lion & Wheel logos. One of only two definitely known GFYE 45s, D25 was economy green, and the other, D26, was lined out. Economy green Peaks were D1/3/5/9/10/2-4/6/25/36/42/6/52/62/3/6/72/8/84/93/5/8, D102/23/5/47/59/63/6/72. (John Ireland)

Opposite above: In the summer of 1966, Toton experimented with a quick-fix repaint and sprayed 20 or so Class 45s into blue. This scheme, known as 'Toton Blue', is the same shade as 'Rail Blue' but, as with WR Hydraulics, the small yellow panels give the illusion of a lighter shade, which is not helped by the matt finish.

Black and white shots can confuse the unwary as both variants had the D-prefixed serif numbering but one giveaway is the lack of any logo on a 'Toton Blue' engine. D71, seen at Leeds City on 29 August 1967, is a fine example. Locos in this style were D47/50/1/5-9/61/4/71/9/91/2, D101/5/9/13/4/6/33/5.

Although not generally listed, I suspect D83 was also a 'Toton Blue' loco but, as it quickly acquired full yellow ends, it is hard to be certain. It did retain the serif numbering and lacked any logo. One other oddity at the time was D24, which was BFYE with a cabside number but in Rail Alphabet style. (Bill Wright)

Opposite below: Compared to almost all the main line classes, very few of the 'Peaks' received FYE on green livery and photos are rare. Four 44s (1,3,6 and 10), just two known 45s (25 and 26) and seven of Class 46 (138, 154, 155, 159, 166, 188 and 193) appeared in the style, despite many lasting in green almost up to TOPS renumbering. Here is D10 Tryfan at Derby Works in December 1972 about to lose the green for blue. Still in traffic in green at this time were 3, 6 and 7, the latter still with small yellow panels. (Bill Ireland)

BR: From Green to Blue

The Toton Blue experiment was not repeated after the summer of 1966 and subsequent repaints from the autumn of that year were in the familiar Rail Blue with full yellow ends that all 193 eventually wore after 1973.

D185 rolls into Stalybridge with the 1100 Liverpool-Newcastle in full Rail Blue, complete with red bufferbeams and an all-blue/grey rake of coaches. This scene is typical of the '70s and early '80s but was actually taken on 10 August 1967, a full year away from the end of BR steam and at a time when Black 5s, 8Fs, 9Fs, WDs Standard 5s and Jubilees were still everyday sights at this location, a modeller's paradise. (Bill Wright)

The classic Rail Blue 'Peak'. Split box headcode 45052 at Cogload on 14 August 1976 with an all-blue/grey rake of mark 1 stock. Coaching stock began to appear in blue/grey from 1965 and maroon coaches had largely disappeared from everyday use by 1971, with the last couple disappearing by 1974. However, there was the famous 'Derby Maroon' set, an entire rake of 12 maroon coaches often trotted out on excursions or on runs to Skegness, but once in September 1974 forming the 1650 Birmingham to Leeds (David Hills)

Class 40

At the TOPS renumbering in May 1973 there were still a great many Class 40s in green livery, all with full yellow ends after the last surviving example with panels, D365, succumbed to Rail Blue in September 1972 whilst still with small yellow panels.

No fewer than 34 examples (40010/7/8/31/5/9/52/87/8/96, 40101/4/6/15/33/5-40/5/9/53/69/71/6/80-4/7/99) ran in green with a TOPS number. Rarest of all for a photo is 40140, which only ran in green for a few weeks at most in 1974. 40039 was withdrawn in 1976 still in the old colours (and considerably more pristine than most) making it one of just three never to run in blue, alongside 40106 and accident victim D322. Already withdrawn, it is seen here dumped at Tinsley on 6 March 1976 next to Rail Blue 40102, also withdrawn at this time. (Chris McKee)

No work on the green to blue changeover period would be complete without a shot of the famous 40106. The last Class 40 in green, it got increasingly tatty and by 25 July 1978 it was in an appalling condition externally, seen here as it takes over the 0715 Nottingham-Glasgow from the inevitable 'Peak' at Leeds City.
  Much time has been spent debating whether it briefly appeared in Rail Blue after its October 1978 overhaul at Crewe and repaint into green. Despite the many sightings by a 'friend of a friend' no proof has ever emerged and I would say such rumours can be safely dismissed as no more than an urban myth. It was repainted into green livery and ran in traffic until April 1983 and is now happily preserved. (Thomas Harper)

The first Class 40 into blue was D237, released from Crewe on 11 May 1967, a few days before the next example D270 on the 21st. Early repaints had serif numbers and an arrow on all four cab sides. None were blue with panels, all being FYE from the first.
  D278 is seen at Kirkcaldy in June 1972, quite recently painted in the standard early 70s pre-TOPS style of Rail Blue. The double arrow is larger than was used on early repaints up till April 1970. After 1973 the size reduced again and later repaints had only arrow per side. (Ian Addison)

40187, at Crewe Works Open Day on 22 September 1979, is in the final style of Rail Blue with a smaller arrow on the driver's cab side. Behind is a new HST set in the first livery of blue, grey and yellow as worn from new in 1976. (Gordon Edgar)

A contrast in Class 40 liveries at Newton Heath. Green 40115 keeps company with a blue classmate. Note the unusual placement of the data panel and the blue stripe denoting a traction motor modification. (Robert Wise)

Class 50

The Class 50s were among the ranks of locomotives delivered in Rail Blue in 1967/8. The D prefix for diesels was dropped as from 14/9/68 although, by then, no steam locos with 4-figure numbers had run in traffic for over 18 months. All 50 50s were delivered with D prefixes and arrows on the cab side below the numbers, but they had mostly lost the D by the early 70s, as seen on 419 at Penrith on 4 March 1972.

D426 was still running around with its prefix as late as December 1973 and it is highly likely that it never lost it. (George Woods)

50031, seen here at Bristol on 7 May 1977, typifies the early style of TOPS numbered 'Hoover'. The old 4xx number is painted out and the 5 figure one applied at the driver's cabside but not at the secondman's side. Prior to TOPS renumbering all 50 retained the cabside arrows, as did many thereafter, with a few receiving a bodyside central arrow upon renumbering. As they were named from 1978 the arrow resumed position on the cabsides at the secondman's side. (Thomas Harper)

D600s

One of the most puzzling aspects of the green to blue changeover is why so many examples of classes clearly earmarked for early withdrawal appeared in blue. The first main line class to disappear was the D600 'Warship' and yet two out of the five examples received blue: D602 is shown here at Plymouth in May 1967 in blue with small yellow panels like other WR hydraulics done at the end of 1966, and more puzzlingly, D600 was given a full Rail Blue repaint complete with FYE in May, a few months before the whole class was switched off on 30 December 1967. (Grahame Wareham)

Contrast in liveries is shown here with the first two members of the class, D600 and D601. D601 remains in green with yellow panels, as did D603 and D604, but D600 is in the aforementioned full Rail Blue it was given just seven months before withdrawal, putting it amongst the list of shortest-lived locomotives in blue. Both are already in the scrap yard at Barry here, where D600 would be broken up in 1970. Staggeringly D601 remained there for a full decade, well into the era of diesel preservation and yet was still scrapped in 1980. (Topticl.com)

Laira on 22 April 1968 sees all 5 of the class on the scrap line. D604 in GSYP leads D601, also GSYP, D602 in BSYP and the third green locomotive no. D603. Just out of view is Rail Blue D600. So an entire class of main line diesel is out of use whilst a couple of hundred miles north, Black 5s, 8Fs, 9Fs and assorted standards could still be seen at work around the Manchester and Preston areas. (The late Keith Holt)

'Warships'

You could easily produce an entire book just including the liveries of the 'Warships'. All were delivered in green livery without panels except for the last few to enter service, D859-65, but thereafter all bets were off. All those built without panels had them applied later as did all but D803 before the fitting of headcode boxes.

Only one loco, the doyen of the class, D800, was scrapped in green (with panels); the rest were either maroon with panels or FYE and various styles of blue. Between September 1965 and October 1966, 32 members of the class were repainted in maroon complete with small yellow panels. The engines concerned were D801/2/5/6/9/11-3/15/7/21/3/8/9/32/4/8-40/2/4/8/55/7/8/61-3/5/7/9/70.

D805 rolls through Totnes light engine on 19 June 1966 in MSYP. In February 1968 it would gain full yellow ends and finally Rail Blue in October 1970, thus appearing in Green with and without panels, maroon with panels and FYE, and Rail Blue FYE. D801/40 were scrapped in maroon with small yellow panels. (Steve Ireland collection)

Many maroon locos also got FYE from August 1967 onwards, such as D812, seen here at Waterloo in April 1969. Note the data panel first applied to locos in autumn 1968, which were always blue regardless of the colour of the engine they were applied to. MFYE 'Warships' were D805/6/9/11/2/5/7/23/9/32/4/8/42/4/69/70. D809/15/7/38 were scrapped in maroon with full yellow ends. Two green engines, numbers D808 and D810, were also given full yellow ends but photographs are scarce indeed. (Grahame Wareham)

Most of the 'Warships' went to blue via differing routes: 64 out of 71 appeared in blue but there were many styles applied. The very first blue 'Warship' was D864 in November 1966 in blue with FYE, serif numbers on the bodyside and cabside arrows. A dispute with PW staff over visibility caused Swindon to outshop many locomotives in blue with yellow panels, including the next two 'Warships' to be done, D830/1. D830 had a cabside number and a central arrow, while D831 had cabside arrows and bodyside numbers.

By May 1967, when it was photographed at Newton Abbot, D864 had already mutated into cabside serif numbers and arrows, its second blue livery in less than nine months following some accident damage which dictated a return to Swindon. Note the burnt umber underframes. (Grahame Wareham)

BR: From Green to Blue

An incredibly rare photo, the only known shot of D848 in green livery without the stripe and with a coaching roundel like a maroon loco seen at Dawlish on 5 March 1966. The engine was probably a depot repaint to cover its poor external condition, done at some point after August 1965. It was a short-lived affair as the loco was repainted maroon a few weeks later. It is unknown if the other side was the same. (Geoff Lendon)

Two distinctive early withdrawals were one of the original trio, D801, and Paxman-engined D830. The former was withdrawn still maroon with panels. D830 was once BSYP and later, in April 1967, was given FYE but retaining the serif numbers which it never lost. D801 was withdrawn in August 1968 and D830 in March 1969. They stand on the scrapline at Laira on 29 August 1969. Both were eventually cut up at Swindon in 1970 and 1971 respectively. (Fred Castor Collection)

Class 52

Many and varied were the colour schemes worn by the 'Westerns', from early experiments in 'Desert Sand', 'Golden Ochre' via Maroon with or without panels and, oddly for a 1960s diesel class, just a few in BR green. The vast majority appeared in maroon at one time or other, perhaps the colour scheme they are most associated with. D1031 seen here at Bristol on 30 August 1965 appeared in only two liveries in its career, maroon with panels and full Rail Blue, but some engines ran in as many as four liveries in as little as eight years. (Bill Wright)

Only six 'Westerns' ever ran in green livery and only three of those never also ran in maroon, numbers 1004/36/7. These three engines went directly to blue, 1004 to full Rail Blue FYE, the other two into the early style with small yellow panels. 1037, seen here at Canton on 21 November 1965, would run like this until January 1967 when it went blue with panels and then Rail Blue from June 1971 in common with the rest of the class. All 74 'Westerns' were eventually BFYE. (John Ireland)

Above: Helen Of Troy's beauty may have launched a thousand ships but this locomotive certainly launched more than a thousand debates. The first blue 'Western', D1030 was released in an odd variation of blue with small arrows, red bufferbeams and small yellow panels, seen here at an open day at Taplow in September 1966. Derby HQ were not impressed and the next 52 to go blue, D1048, was in standard Rail Blue with FYE. A dispute over visibility for PW staff then caused Swindon to outshop several hydraulic classes in blue but with panels. Westerns concerned were 1030/6/7/43/7/57.

None of that has caused as much controversy as the shade of blue, often referred to as 'Chromatic Blue'. Now I am going to ruffle a few feathers and just say it is exactly the same shade as Rail Blue. Only the method of application (sprayed not brushed) and the optical illusion created by the SYP fools the eye and of course the various shades of colour film emulsion do not help. I'll just close by saying the van behind the loco is in exactly the same shade... (Grahame Wareham)

Opposite above: Several maroon locos had FYE applied from summer 1967 including D1001, seen next to a full Rail Blue D1022 at Bath Road in June 1968. D1022 had been BFYE since the previous July but D1001 had only worn MFYE for one month at the time of this shot. Others were 1002/8/12/6/25/39/41/4/5/54/6/67/8.

For a short period at the end of 1966 and early 1967 it was possible to see green, maroon and blue 'Westerns' with panels and one in full Rail Blue. The last green example went blue just before the first maroon ones got FYE, which is a pity. (Grahame Wareham)

Class 47

The 512 Class 47s, with the exception of D1733 (of which more later) and the last handful to enter traffic in 1966/7, D1953-61, were all delivered in two-tone green with small yellow panels, as seen here with D1610 at Salisbury on 29 August 1964. This was a comparatively short-lived state of affairs as full yellow ends for all locomotives became mandatory from February 1967 and the 47s very quickly had them added, commencing in March 1967 with D1849. The last to run in the style was D1744, losing them at its repaint to Rail Blue in November 1970, by which time well over 100 had already gone blue and the rest were in GFYE. (David Christie)

Above: Where Rail Blue all began. In 1964, British Railways tried out a new 'corporate' image, part of which involved a new standard livery to be applied to all locomotives and rolling stock. The first attempt was branded 'XP64', comprising a specially liveried Class 47 with matching stock, which toured the country to gauge public reaction and opinions.

Newly built (and still in primer) D1733 was the selected loco, sent to Derby on 16 July 1964 for painting in the new colours. Initially the double arrow backed with red was applied to all four cabsides but was removed soon after the publicity tour ended. The engine then worked as a normal 47 and was eventually taken into standard Rail Blue in 1969. It is seen here entering Paddington with a mixed livery rake of mark 1s, the leading vehicle in the revived GWR chocolate and cream livery, on 20 September 1964. (David Christie)

Opposite above: There were several different styles of Rail Blue applied to the 47s. The new builds in blue, D1953-61, had cabside arrows and numbers on the body behind the cab doors, as shown here by 47514, the former D1960 at Holyhead on 21 July 1974.

Most of them went into standard Rail Blue in 1973 but D1956 briefly became 47260 and retained the cabside arrows for a while after renumbering, from February to July 1974. It then went into Crewe Works for ETH fitting, emerging as 47553. 47514 stayed in this style for some time afterwards, finally conforming in October 1975. (Mel Jones, Steve Ireland Collection)

Opposite below: Early repaints from green to blue in 1967/8 were slightly different to those built in blue with cabside numbers (D prefixed at first) and bodyside arrows. D1528, seen here at Ipswich on 15 January 1968 just two months after repaint at Crewe in November 1967, was the first to appear, followed by D1531/2/6/47/50/8/69/75/95, D1692, D1723/5 and D1932 before the D prefix was discarded in September 1968. A few more followed in the style (minus D) with 1662/84, 1712/8 going blue before the change to the standard central body arrow and bodyside number arrangement began in December 1968 with 1649. (Bill Wright)

BR: From Green to Blue

Above: The style beloved of spotters of my generation, the classic two tone GFYE 47, worn here by the former D1869, now renumbered 47219, at Gateshead on 19 August 1974.

47s easily dominated the numbers of main line green TOPS locos. Known for certain are 47033/41/50/2/60/1/91/4/9, 47109/21/6/9/31/7/8/46/8/52/70/1/3/5/8/82/3/7-91/5, 47201/3/4/6-8/10/3-24/7/32/7/56/62/4/7/8/71/83/97, 47310/1/3/8/22/4/33/5/40/7/53/4/6-60/2-7/9/70/4/6/9/80, 47494, 47520/2/3/5-7 and possibly 47125/84, 47205/12, 47319. (Ian Addison)

Opposite above: The very last Class 47 to go blue was 47256 which, alongside 47365/6, survived long enough to gain the domino style headcodes applied to many locos after 1976. Here it is at Immingham on 19 June 1977 in the company of a couple of blue classmates. A few months later the loco suffered fire damage and was repainted in an odd all-over green livery with red bufferbeams which it wore until finally going blue, nearly a year after the next last to do so, in September 1978. (Thomas Harper)

Opposite below: The Queen's Silver Jubilee in June 1977 prompted Stratford to paint Union Jacks on the sides of two of their 47s, numbers 47163/4. As the rail mags then were about a month or so behind events our little gang of teenage spotters were most surprised to see these two engines roaring through the local line on the Harwich-Manchester 'Boat train', our sole source of SF-based engines in Nottinghamshire. This action opened the gates for more sheds to personalize their engines later on. 47164 is seen here at Sheffield in September 1977 having run round the 'Boat Train' prior to departing for Manchester. (George Woods)

BR: From Green to Blue

A standard Rail Blue Class 47, albeit one of the highly prized 'namers', 47077 *North Star*, is seen at Birmingham New Street on 29 July 1978. The style of bodyside number and a central arrow was worn at the time by all the class bar 47256 which remained in its unique all-over green livery.

Just four of the class never ran in this livery variation, the four early accident-damaged examples listed elsewhere. (David Hills)

Class 03

Standard green liveried Class 03 D2134 is seen here stabled at Laira on 3 September 1972. The whole class were delivered in green and at first had no 'wasp stripes', later retro-added to all the class. The Gill Sans numbering was replaced on some green locos by serif style.

121 of the class lasted long enough to get a TOPS number, three of which were green at the time, including D2134. The other two were 03128 and 03382. Only 03382 went to blue and not until 1979. The other two were both taken out of service in green. D2048/51/3/6 at least were given arrows on green, a Doncaster Works practice. (John Ireland)

The standard Rail Blue Class 03 in the shape of 03386 at Derby Works open day on 4 Sept 1976. Unusually it appears to be lacking a data panel on the cab. The loco was already withdrawn at the time of this shot just prior to the withdrawal of green 03128/34, leaving 03382 to carry on in green for three more years. (David Hills)

Class 04

The Class 04s were originally delivered in black, with later examples in green. Most were withdrawn in green (some with double arrows) but a handful of this class ran in Rail Blue from 1967 despite their impending withdrawal. The locos concerned were D2200/9/11/31/9/58/93-5. It is not know for sure but possible that a few may have gone to blue from black and escaped the green stage altogether.

D2258 survived in Rail Blue for many years after withdrawal and sale in 1970 and was used at various industrial locations including Bennerley Disposal Point near Ilkeston, where it is seen on 26 July 1979.
A few miles north of here, green liveried 03 D2138 (in the same style as D2134 illustrated elsewhere in this book) was also in industrial use at Pye Hill colliery, and Rail Blue 03037 was at West Hallam. (Pete Wilcox)

Class 06

In common with most non-standard classes of shunter, the 35 Class 06s were mainly withdrawn in green but a handful did make it to blue and also to TOPS renumbering. Here is 06006 which was repainted blue in August 1967 as D2423 and survived in traffic until 1980, near the end of its working days at Dundee Harbour on 18 July 1979.

A few more, 2414/20-2/6/37/40, followed suit prior to TOPS renumbering, encompassing ten survivors in 1973; eight blue and two green. Some report D2434 as also being Rail Blue but not surviving to TOPS, which I think is unlikely but, if I have learned one thing from studying this topic, it is that nothing can be taken for granted! (Bill Atkinson)

Of the ten Class 06s that made it to TOPS, the first and last of the batch, 06001/10, remained green for a while, 06010 until withdrawal in June 1975. 06001, however, was given a coat of Rail Blue in May 1975 and ran for a little over a year longer in traffic until September 1976, which does seem rather a waste of money, especially as it was quickly scrapped by Campbell's of Airdrie in 1977. Here it is on 3 August 1974 in the company of Blue 06004 at Eastfield. (Bill Ireland)

Class 05

Many hundreds of diesel shunting locomotives of many different designs abounded in the 50s and 60s, the vast majority of which were withdrawn long before TOPS numbering and in the main before Rail Blue.
 Class 05 D2581, seen here at Thornton Junction on 16 July 1965, is a good example. Of the 69 locos of this type, only one got Rail Blue, number D2554, and that only because it was transferred to the IOW and thus outlived its classmates by over a decade. D2581, in common with the rest of the class (barring the aforementioned D2554), did not even outlive steam, being withdrawn in June 1968 and scrapped not long after, still green. (Bill Wright)

Class 01

The small Class 01s remained in the original black livery to the end of their lives. Two locos, D2954/5, were retained to work on the Holyhead Breakwater until 1979 and 1981 respectively and renumbered 01001/2. 01002, the former D2955, rests inside the shed at Holyhead on 12 Sept 1979.

Oddly they were not the only locos to remain black into TOPS numbering. Willesden's D3052, allocated 08039 but withdrawn in December 1973 before it ever carried it, was black to the end of its life. But 08105 was renumbered whilst black and lasted until 1975 in that colour. (Bill Atkinson)

Class 02

None of the 20-strong class of 02 shunters ever ran in blue. D2850, seen here at Allerton in April 1969, was only to survive until June 1970 anyway but the three that did last long enough to be renumbered differed from this solely in having their TOPS numbers 02001/3/4 applied instead of the D28xx ones. D2852 was allocated 02002 but withdrawn in October 1973 before it had chance to get it. (TopTicl.com)

Unclass

Another class that disappeared before the end of steam and just before the classification system was the 73-strong class of shunters built by NBL, numbers D2708-80. None ever appeared in blue despite other minor classes having the odd member do so. D2729, minus rods despite withdrawal not being for a few months yet, stands at Perth in August 1966. It looks in pretty good external condition suggesting a recent overhaul but it is likely it never turned a wheel in anger again. An oddity in this class was D2709 which had a coaching roundel as opposed to a lion and wheel. (Charlie Cross-Gordon Edgar collection)

D2913, seen at Rugby, was a member of a similar NBL-built shunter class. Despite the late date of 29 July 1965 it remains in black without any wasp stripes. Other members of the class did get wasp stripes and also green livery. (Bill Wright)

Class 07

Another small class of shunters was Class 07. Unusually all 14 not only survived into the late 70s but every example was repainted Rail Blue. The original green livery is shown by D2998, the last of its class, at Eastleigh on 5 June 1967. Green examples had the coaching stock roundel as seen here, the same as applied to a few Class 20s and Class 33 D6570 amongst others. This engine was one of few that received Rail Blue whilst D prefixes were in use and it never lost it, although not withdrawn until May 1973. (Bill Wright)

The usual style for Rail Blue on Class 07 was, as shown here, with cabside number and arrow and the post-1968 data panel. This loco, 2997, is minus a D prefix indicating a repaint post-September 1968, or possibly a second trip to works, although that is unlikely as it received its TOPS number 07013 in December 1973.

D2988 was different in that the arrow was above the number. The position of the data panel varied depending on the loco. (Unknown Photographer)

Class 08/9/10/3

Class 08 D3052, seen here withdrawn at Willesden on 25 July 1974, is still in black livery as delivered, suggesting that, barring the addition of wasp stripes, it was never repainted in its 19-year career on BR. Allocated 08039 in the May 1973 renumbering scheme for diesels, it was withdrawn in December before it could carry it (although it can be seen chalked on the cabside).

The first few hundred of this class appeared in black livery from 1952, later to go green from 1960 on. It is surprising enough that the engine lasted into the mid-70s in black but more surprising still is that classmate D3170 actually got renumbered 08105, also still black, and lasted until repainted blue in 1975. (Ray Honke 'Mr Deltic')

D4159, seen at Laira on 29 August 1969, wears the standard livery for the 1193-strong fleet of Class08/9/10 and non-class 0-6-0 shunters of green with red coupling rods and the wasp stripes applied from 1960, possibly starting with D3963 from new and then added to most afterwards. D3683 was minus the stripes as late as 1969 when seen at Chester. LMR Works generally put the lion on the battery boxes as seen here, ER ones on the bodyside. (Fred Castor collection)

Above: A major attraction for us 1970s spotters in the East Midlands was the line of 08s waiting to be admitted into or released back to traffic from Derby Works. Often these engines would be from far flung outposts of BR and a good source of 'cops'. No such luck with 3570, newly ex-works on 1 September 1972, for it was a Derby allocated engine.
  Blue livery varied, as with other classes, according to the works that did the work, although this style was easily the most common with the central arrow and yellow coupling rods. (John Evans)

Opposite above: There were many, many variations of blue on Class 08s, some with cabside arrows and numbers, others with cabside number and arrow elsewhere, red, yellow or unpainted rods and so on. 08723 was a particularly odd example with its serif numbers and black coupling rods, seen at Hamilton on 23 May 1976. 08779 was another serif example. The vast majority had the Rail Alphabet style. (Trevor Hall)

Opposite below: At the beginning of the TOPS renumbering in May 1973 there were still a great many 08s and 09s in green livery (as well as a handful in black), totalling over 270 locomotives. By 1973 all the non-standard designs, 146 Class 10s and the unclassified engines D3117-26 and D3152-66, totalling 171 locomotives had been withdrawn, only three of which had made it to Rail Blue; Class 10s D3138, 3638 and 4078.
  In addition, some of the early 08s had been withdrawn in 1972/3 while still green, and even a few that made it to TOPS numbering never wore Rail Blue, numbers 08010/43/57/65/6, 08135/7, 08229, 08306/7/10/57/8 and 08566, plus maybe 08267 and one or two others. 08911, seen here at Carlise on 20 August 1974, has been recently renumbered and just has the old number painted out in green and the new applied over the top. Some had a blue background rather than green. (Ian Addison)

BR: From Green to Blue

Above: A celebrity green 08 before it became a celebrity. Battered green 08531 stands at its home depot of Stratford on 28 May 1977. It was shortly to be repainted into shiny green and used as Liverpool Street Pilot for several years. Stratford tradition dictated that the Liverpool Street Pilot was always in immaculate condition. or a time in the early 1970s the job fell to Class 15 number 8234. (David Hills)

Opposite above: A contrast in blue 08 styles with Longsight's 08914 and 915 on 11 April 1980. 08914 is in the standard scheme with yellow coupling roads and yellow bufferbeam but 08915 retains a little of what was dubbed 'Longsight Blue' with red bufferbeams and rods and a slightly different shade of blue livery. Longsight applied this to a few locos in 1971 with hand-lettered numbers above the arrows on the cabside. Both these engines wore that livery as D4144/5, as did D3776/72/8/84, 3853, 4136. 4144 had a reversed double arrow on one cab which it kept as 08914 for a while. (David Hills)

Opposite below: 09005, seen here at Clapham Jn in 1974, does not appear to know what livery it is in, complete with arrows and lion, and red and yellow coupling rods. Two other 09s remained in green long enough to get TOPS numbers 09024/5 were the locos concerned. (TopTicl.com)

BR: From Green to Blue

The three Class 13 'master and slave' locos converted from Class 08s in 1965 were all in green at the time of the conversion and remained so until 1972 when D4500 got a coat of Rail Blue. The other two remained green into TOPS as 13001/2. 13001 went blue in 1974 but 13002 lingered on in battered green until 1977. Here it is at Tinsley in September 1976. (John Woolley)

13001 stands at Tinsley on 12 July 1981 in standard Rail Blue with yellow coupling rods as you would expect for this era. By 1981 there were no green locomotives in capital stock if you do not count the celebrity repaints 40106 and co., but a few did linger on in departmental use as Class 15s converted to carriage heating units. In fact, there never was a point when all of BR's fleet was standard blue. (Roger Norton)

Class 24

All the Class 24s were delivered in green without panels. Uniquely liveried D5000, with its waist-level pale blue stripe, is seen at Aylesbury on 3 Sept 1966. It is a shame that just this engine out of the 151 Class 24s had this as in my opinion it was a very attractive style. Notice the cabside numbers are also set lower down than normal and the different siting of the lion and wheel. D5000 remained in this one-off livery until repainted in blue in early 1970 when it became just another blue 24, becoming 24005 in 1974. (George Woods)

An interesting pairing of D5009 in GSYP and D5005 in the two-tone green applied to a handful of the class in 1965, the engines concerned being D5005/7/8/40/53/72. After this shot was taken at Olney on 23 March 1967, these two had widely differing futures. 5009, mundanely, was repainted blue in 1971 and went to Scotland to work out its career, with its one minor claim to fame being that it was the last 24 overhauled at Glasgow, a few months before withdrawal. 5005 was withdrawn in January 1969 but its body was 'donated' to 5025 which was then scrapped. So 5005 became 5025, acquired blue livery (initially with cabside arrows and bodyside numbers) and later became 24025 until it too was scrapped in January 1977. (John Evans)

Another two-tone green repaint, D5037 complete with FYE, is seen at Cockshute in December 1972 not long before repaint in Rail Blue and renumbering to 24037. Other two-tone green 24s that received FYE were 5038, 5053 and 5072. None survived to TOPS in two-tone green sadly. (John Ireland)

A fair number of Class 24 got a TOPS number whilst still in Green, 24032/5/9/47/57/63/81/2/90/2/4, 24136/42/7. Three were never repainted blue, 24090/2 and 24136, two of which are shown here on the dump at Swindon in 1976. 24092 is green but has a double arrow symbol as did a few other members of the class. D5113 had one whilst still GSYP and TOPS numbered 24081. Other Class 24s to escape Rail Blue but withdrawn prior to TOPS were D5005, 5051, 5067, 5088, 5093, 5122, 5139 and 5149 with the possibility of 5043. (John Ireland)

Besides green locomotives with arrows there were the opposite, blue locos with lion and wheel logos. 5021 never lost the lion even as 24021 and was finally withdrawn in the style in August 1975. Its initial repaint to blue in 1966 is thought to have been with SYP in the same style as Class 25 D5218. Another early blue peculiarity was D5026, repainted blue with SYP albeit with Rail Alphabet numbers and cabside arrows, running in traffic from late 1966 to the start of 1971.

24021 stands on the scrap line at Reddish on 29 August 1976. (David Hills)

Green 24136 and blue 24049 double-head a freight at Dee Marsh in 1975. By this time the sight of differently coloured locos double-heading was not common except for the pairs of 20s that proliferated in the East Midlands. Moreover, these two engines had differing front ends as 24136 was one of the later batch from D5114 that had headcode panels over the front windows. (David Hills)

Above: The standard style for the Rail Blue Class 24, as for the standard Rail Blue Class 25, was the central arrow and cabside arrows which most of the class appeared in.

    5024 is seen on 11 May 1973, looking very new and modern livery-wise amid the ramshackle LMS glory of Manchester Victoria, which probably never saw a lick of paint once during the whole of BR era. (John Evans)

Opposite above: Many Class 24s received GFYE, including Gateshead's 5103 and 5110, shown climbing away from Pelaw South Junction on 30 September 1970 with a Tyne Dock-Consett Iron Ore working. Both retain the pleasing white stripe along the bottom of the bodyside and serif numbers. Many lost the lining for a less aesthetically appealing plain green.

    5110 as 24110 is frequently listed amongst the ranks of Green TOPS Class 24s but I have to say no proof exists to say either way. Whatever the truth, both these engines ran in green up till the onset of TOPS numbering, and both did go Rail Blue. (Bill Jamieson)

Opposite below: Inverurie Works had an easily spotted style of repainting locomotives into blue, having serif style numbers with the arrows usually applied to the cab doors. By August 1971, Inverurie-painted Class 24 D5117's arrows had migrated to the bodyside, possibly due to replacement of doors although the serif D prefixed number remains in situ. It was not uncommon to see blue locos with green cab doors and vice versa as little thought was given to the overall effect if work needed to be done. Behind D5117 is Glasgow Works repaint Class 26 D5345, done in March 1968, so also with a D prefix but Rail Alphabet numbering. (Grahame Wareham)

BR: From Green to Blue

Class 25

Above: D7671, just six months old and in blue with FYE, looking as delivered from new, stands at Kingmoor on 2 August 1967. D7669, of the previous batch, was renumbered to 25319, retaining this style as late as 1975. Early green to blue repaints roughly adopted this style, with the position of the numbers being further away from the edge of the grille and the cabside depending which end they were. However, the first Class 25 to receive blue livery in 1966 was D5218 which was blue with SYP, serif style numbers and a lion and wheel. It ran until August 1971 in the style moreover. Next to it is one of the two Class 28 'Co-Bos' that ran in green with FYE, no D5707. The other was D5708 which was far more camera shy. (David Quayle)

Opposite above: Class 25s were of two differing body designs, one like the Class 24 and others, like this shot of D7661, which were delivered in two tone green. The last few into traffic were delivered in Rail Blue with cabside arrows and D prefixed numbers on the bodyside. D7660/1, new at the end of 1966 even had small yellow panels as shown here with D7661 at Willesden in August 1969. D7660 had already assumed standard blue to previous year but D7661 was to run until 1970 in the style. (Grahame Wareham)

Opposite below: Several Class 25s of both body design styles survived in green long enough to wear TOPS numbers: 25036/8/40/3/53/4/8, 25102, 25202/3/18/48/51/2/60/1/76/8/85/94, 25305, and perhaps a few others that cannot be confirmed with photo evidence.

25218 stands at St Pancras in 1974 in poor external condition. Its bodyside stripe has all but worn away and the loco is devoid of any logo. Others were in better external nick (and odd ones worse!)

25102 was the last survivor in green until April 1976. Only two never made it to Rail Blue, accident damage victims 5278 and 7605, which were both withdrawn in GFYE. (Paul Haywood).

BR: From Green to Blue

Above: The standard Rail Blue Class 25 is illustrated here by 25175 at Stafford on 15 June 1985, with cabside number and a central bodyside arrow. Many locos had the number applied to the bodyside also. The lengthy parcels train is of interest too, though a few years previously would have seen a far wider variety of vehicles and liveries, not just mundane BG and CCT vans but also GW siphons, SR 'S' vans and LMS CCTs and BGs. (Russell Saxton)

Opposite: 7647 trundles through Melton Mowbray with a mixed freight, in a scene that could be anytime from 1964 onwards but is in fact 7 July 1972, long past the time when FYE for all locos was mandatory. A few 25s ran with panels right up to the moment of renumbering, D7600/59 until February 1974 and admission to Crewe. D7600 even had a chalked-on number 25250.

No Class 25 or, in fact, any other loco ran in green or blue with a yellow panel as TOPS but it was a near miss for some. D7564 had a double arrow on two tone green livery for a while, believed unique for this class. (John Evans)

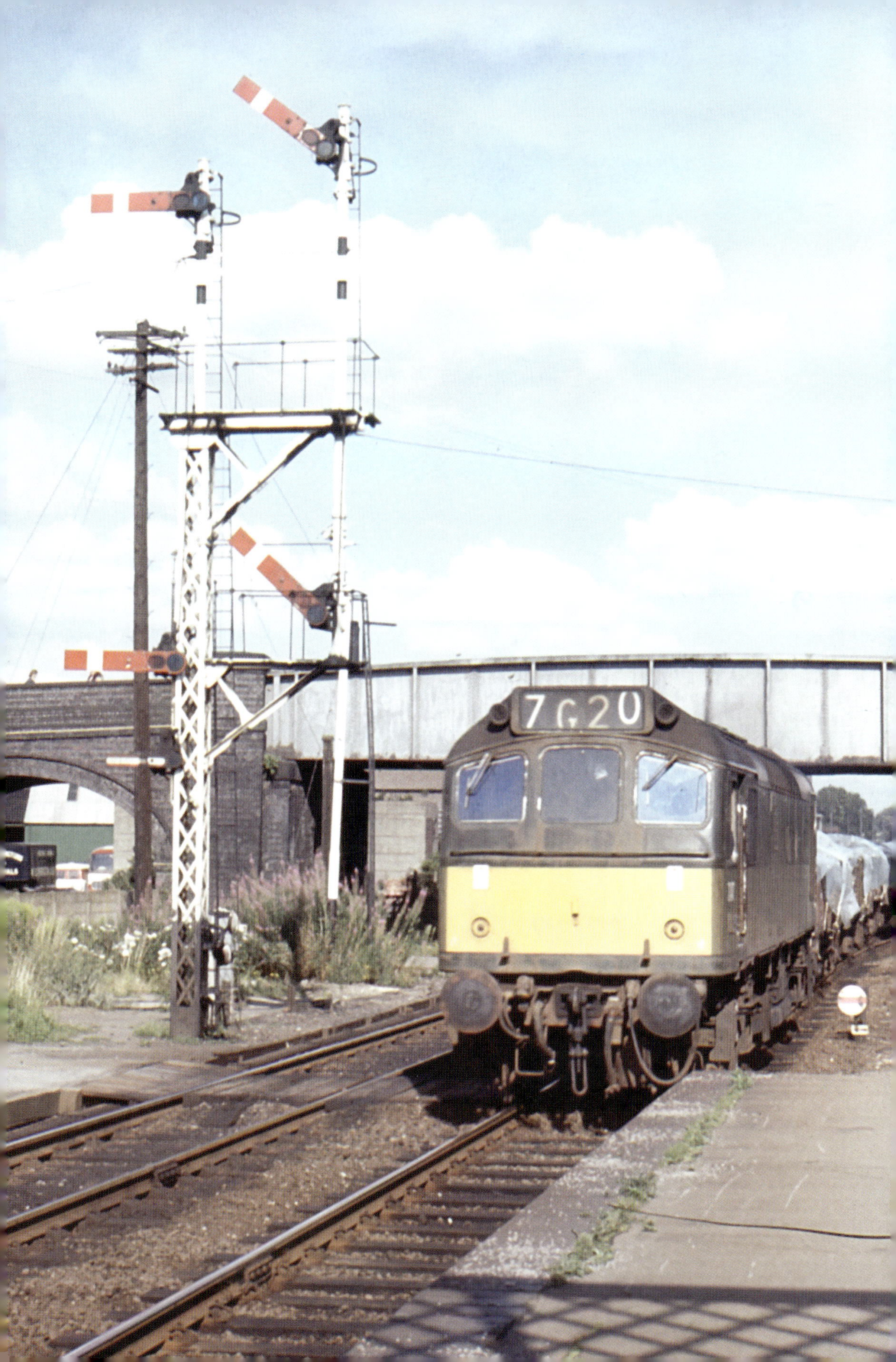
7G20

Class 26

The Class 26 locomotives were repainted into blue livery quite early on and few remained in green by 1970. Only one engine got full yellow ends on green, D5335. Initially, as seen here at Inverness on 6 August 1969, it was lined out like all 26s were at first but later on it (also uniquely for a Class 26) lost the lining and ran for years in plain green with no D prefix. (Gordon Edgar)

5335 again in a doubly unique livery for a Class 26. Green with full yellow ends was already a one-off but later on it lost the lining and ran in the style shown here, until its inevitable repaint to Rail Blue. There were never any other unlined Class 26s and, as mentioned, just this one with GFYE. It had lost the D but interestingly retained the serif numbering. It had already outlasted almost all its classmates in green by 14 October 1971 when it was photographed at Kyle Of Localsh waiting to depart for Inverness with a peculiar hybrid parcels and passenger train, typical of the route. (George Woods)

Blue repaints for Class 26s varied in style. The first into blue was D5343, done by Inverurie with serif numbers on the cab as usual and arrows on the cab doors, like D5117 shown elsewhere in this book. Glasgow then did a batch in April 1967 with Rail Alphabet numbers on the bodyside and cabside arrows, numbers D5304/5/7/11/20/7/31/6/42. Subsequent repaints had cabside numbers and a bodyside arrow, as seen here on 5303 at Haymarket in August 1971. The cabside windows were left blue on the repaints but later on, after 1971, the yellow was extended around them too. The vast majority were done before the end of steam and had D prefixes. Very few survived into the 1970s in green. (Grahame Wareham)

Class 27

Class 27s up to D5368 were delivered from new in lined green without yellow panels, possibly up to D5369, although I can find no proof at the time of writing.

D5350, seen here at Eastfield, shows the style worn by the whole class eventually, of lined out green with SYP. Class 27s lasted far longer than Class 26s in green and several lasted into 1973/4, with two making it to TOPS as 27001/24. On the right is Class 20 D8079 which has not yet received any kind of yellow on the cab fronts. Several Class 20s were like this as late as 1968, especially on the ScR (Charlie Cross-Gordon Edgar Collection)

Green SYP Class 27 D5373 and early blue Class 25 D5202 face to face at Toton in late 1967. Neither have yet had the data panels listing class, weight, route availability etc. applied, as they would from 1968, and D5202 still wears the M under its number denoting its allocation (David Hills)

The first Class 27 into blue, D5389, was done by Derby in 1966 in a totally unique style for the class of small yellow panels and bodyside numbers with the arrows on the cab. It ran like this for several years but photos are scarce. It was still in the livery at Dundee Tay Bridge in August 1970 at any rate. By now it had lost the D prefixes and it is thought it lost them before leaving the LMR for the ScR in November 1969. (Grahame Wareham)

Two Class 27s, D5380/2, were given a coat of two-tone green in 1966 by Derby whilst they were based on the LMR. Both migrated to the ScR in the late 60s and D5382 quickly went blue in the late summer of 1968. D5380, however, received FYE and ran on until 1971 and the inevitable coat of blue. In a very grimy state, the engine is seen here among the unreconstructed steam-era glory of Polmadie in August 1971. Note that the loco's cabside windows are painted yellow. (Grahame Wareham)

D5406, at Polmadie again in August 1971, has had an arrow symbol applied whilst still in green livery. This was the usual practice of Doncaster Works, although I don't think they were guilty on this occasion.
 Examples of class 03, 04, 08, 11, 12, 15, 16, 20, 23, 24, 25, 27, 31, 37 and 55 all ran in green with arrows. D5406 ran like this right up till its repaint into blue in late 1973 but it was outlived by several 24s, 31s and 37s. Note that it retains the white cab window surrounds. (Grahame Wareham)

Two Class 27s survived in green as TOPS numbered examples, 27001/24. 27024, the former D5370, had lost its attractive lining and was in plain green but happily D5347, as 27001, remained in the full lined out green with full yellow ends, seen here at Glasgow Queen Street on 22 August 1974. (Ian Addison)

The final style of Rail Blue worn by Classes 26 and 27 was a bodyside number and central arrows with the yellow extended around the cabside windows, as seen here on 27203 at Haymarket on 11 November 1978. Only one 27 was never painted blue, accident victim D5383, scrapped in green with small yellow panels. (David Hills)

Class 31

Most Class 31s were delivered in lined green, minus any yellow panels. The first new build to have them was D5828 in 1962. The whole class had SYP applied retroactively from 1962. D5656 typifies the early style, here at York with a stopper for Doncaster in May 1962, not long after being given small yellow panels. Notice the rake of maroon LNER design stock, still very common at the time. There were several variations: a great many had FYE, some with arrows, others with lion and wheel logos, and there were serif and Rail Alphabet numbers both with and without D prefixes.

The last 31 into blue was 5818 in May 1974 but just before this 5827 had the distinction of being the only 31 to run in green with a TOPS number as 31294 for about three weeks in February and March. (Grahame Wareham)

D5578 and D5579 were delivered in experimental colour schemes, D5578 in blue and D5579 in Golden Ochre. Neither livery was classed as much of a success and D5578 quickly went into standard GSYP in September 1964 with D5579 following in February 1966. D5578 is seen here at Derby not long before it went the opposite way to most, from blue to green at Derby on 4 July 1964. One interesting point is the 'Blue Star' coupling codes, normally applied onto a yellow end, have had to be surrounded by white circles so as to be seen. There is a prototype, as they say, for everything! (John Ireland)

Above: The first 31 into Rail Blue in October 1966 was D5649, and it remained the only example for almost a year until D5857 opened the flood in 1967. Initial blue repaints had cabside arrows and numbers on the bodyside and all locos done up to April 1971 were in this style. Later repaints had the number on the cab and a central arrow on the body. D5649's number style was different to all the subsequent examples, as can be seen here in this shot of it ex-works at Doncaster in October 1966. (Grahame Wareham)

Opposite above: Blue repaints for Class 31s up till September 1968 all had D prefixes in common with all the diesels with numbers below 9999 (and a few above!). Later examples such as 5595, seen here at King's Cross in September 1969, did not have them applied. The first coach behind the engine is a maroon liveried Mark 1, vanishing rapidly by this time. (Grahame Wareham)

Opposite below: After mid-1971 Class 31 repaints to blue followed the style shown here by 31227, pictured at Peterborough on 5 March 1977, with a cabside number and central arrow. The train is of equal interest, comprising parcels vans of BR, SR, LMS and GWR origins, all of course in Rail Blue! However, 45 locos remained in the older style long enough to gain TOPS numbers, the engines concerned being 31002/06/13, 31107/111/113/115/120/126/128/ 129/132/134/135/140/145/146/147/149/150/153/154/156/157/158/164/169/172/192/197/210/216/217/224/ 226/232/244/251/256/258/259/303/304/306/307/310/311/312/321/325 & 408, the last listed having arrows on the secondman's side and the number on the driver's cabside. 31256/8/9 were in a style dubbed 'Old Oak style' with the number squeezed in above the arrow on the cab. (Stuart Ray)

52

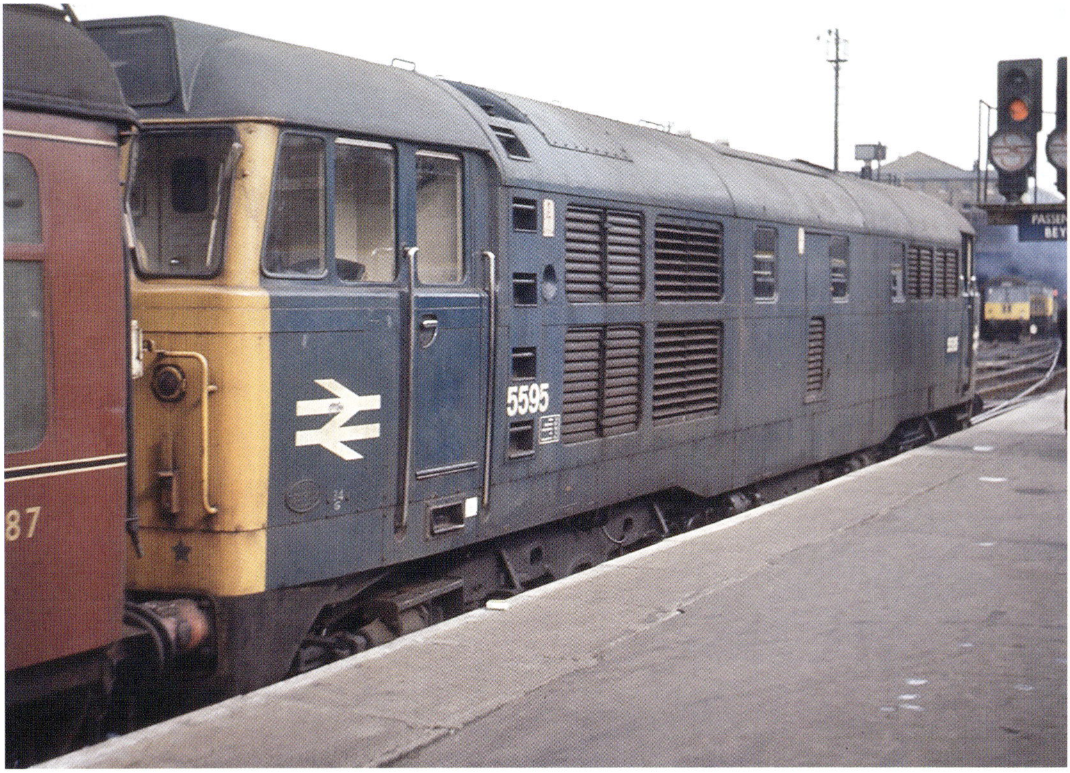
5595

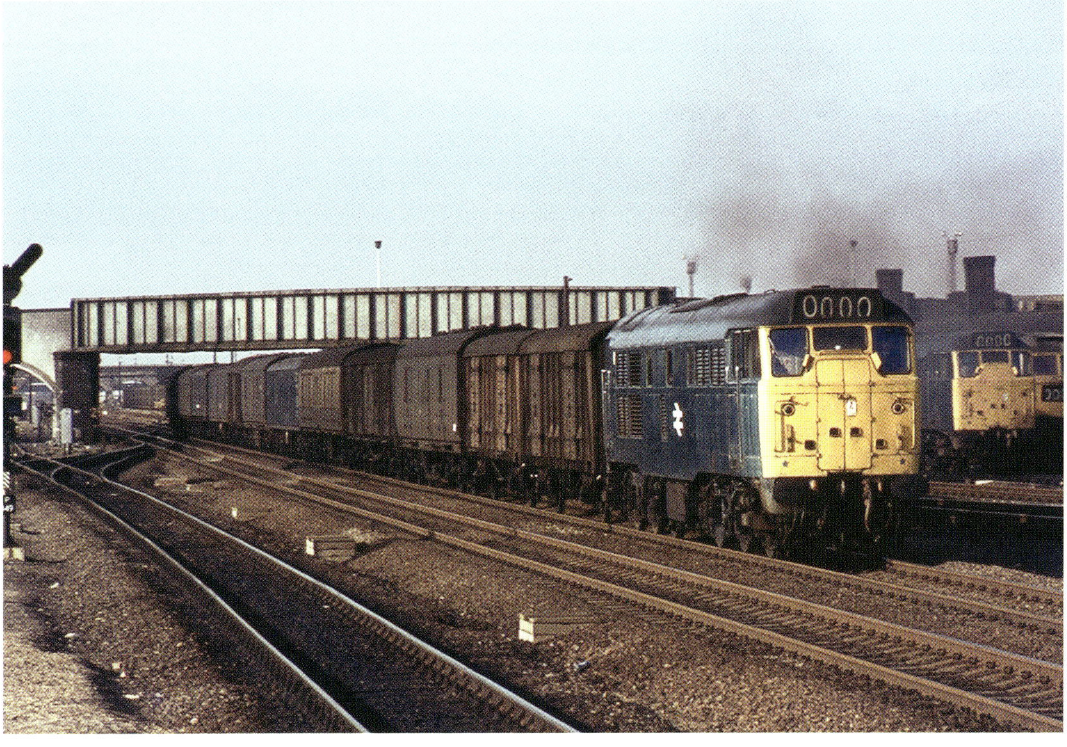

Class 28

A real puzzler is the repainting into Rail Blue of a CoBo Class 28. The writing was on the wall for this small class of 20 non-standard engines long before June 1967, when D5701 got a full repaint into Rail Blue at Crewe Works. Despite the imminent end of steam there appears to be a large number of photos of this engine during its short period of use in blue. Here it is at Carnforth on 25 June 1968, a few weeks away from withdrawal in September. A shame it was not also preserved given that it had recently been overhauled, although the survival of D5705 is, in itself, a miracle. (Bill Wright)

Class 23

Originally delivered in green with a white lower body stripe and no panels, the 'Baby Deltics' were taken out of service after a few years in an attempt to rectify their awful reliability. When they re-emerged in 1964/5, they sported a pale green lower body stripe, headcode boxes and yellow panels, a much more pleasing effect. D5900/3/4/8 had full yellow ends applied from 1967 and D5908 was given the Doncaster-style arrow on green livery.

D5902 is shown at Stratford 7 June 1970. Behind the engine is Class 11 12106, green like most of its classmates, although a few did sneak into blue. (Gordon Edgar)

The 'Baby Deltics' also featured a rogue repaint to Rail Blue in the form of D5909 done at Doncaster in February 1968, reputedly due to collision damage. Here it is dumped at Stratford in September 1971 where it would linger until 1973 before scrapping at Cohen's of Kettering. It and its classmates were outlasted by several years by D5901, transferred to Derby Test Centre and given a temporary reprieve until 1975 when it was replaced by a Class 24. (Grahame Wareham)

Class 21

Most certainly not one BR's success stories, the NBL type 2s, later classified 21, had short lives mostly dumped out of service. Twenty were converted to Class 29s but the remaining 38 were all withdrawn by late 1968. Originally all-over green, most received yellow panels after 1962 but at least D6125 and D6127, which suffered fire damage in 1962 and never ran again, did not.

D6142, shown here at Inverurie in May 1966, shows the default livery style for the Class 21-but one made it into Rail Blue! (Charlie Cross-Gordon Edgar collection).

Class 29

Twenty of the spectacularly unsuccessful NBL Class 21s were re-engined and re-classifield Class 29 and survived a few years longer. The livery was changed to a two-tone green with yellow panels. Headcode panels were also fitted, except to the first to be so treated, D6123.
  D6132 stands at Inverurie in June 1968. The loco is yet to receive a data panel and still has the steam-era 65A (Eastfield) shedplate. (Grahame Wareham)

Although the reprieve granted by refurbishment was short, all the Class 29s that did not receive blue livery eventually got FYE, including the sole disc-fitted example 6123, seen here at Perth on 9 April 1970. By now it is minus D prefix but with data panel and red circle coupling code common to Class 16, 21, 28, 29 and, oddly, Class 31/0 'Toffee-apples'. As with most photos of this time the coaching stock is of great interest, a mix of maroon and blue/grey. Maroon stock was becoming thin on the ground by now but would outlast 6123 and all its classmates in service. (Bill Jamieson)

A handful of the Class 29s (and one Class 21) ran in Rail Blue. Inverurie repainted them in its particular style shown here by 6137 at Polmadie in August 1971. 6100/7/8/19/24/9/37 all ran in blue along with D6109 from Class 21, which was modified externally to become a Class 29, complete with headcode panel but not re-engined. D6109 did not last long in traffic and made the unusual, but far from unknown, sight of a Rail Blue diesel on the scrap line at the same time as steam locomotives. (Grahame Wareham)

Class 22

The NBL diesel hydraulic class 22s were delivered in green without yellow panels up till D6336, thereafter from new. Just over half were never repainted blue but, despite many green examples lasting to the end of the class, only D6312/31 ever received full yellow ends. This is 6323 seen at Oxford in June 1969, one of just two green machines to lose the D prefix, the other being 6352. (Grahame Wareham)

The first four Class 22s repainted into blue were in the peculiar style adopted by the WR during a short-lived dispute of visibility for PW men in late 1966. D6300/3/14/27 were outshopped in blue with serif numbers and yellow panels. The arrow positions on D6314/27 were different on each side to add confusion. D6300/3 were quickly withdrawn in May 1968 and D6314 in April 1969 but D6327, seen here at Old Oak in April 1969, soldiered on in this livery until withdrawal in May 1971. (Grahame Wareham)

Several Class 22s received standard Rail Blue in 1967, easily spotted by the cabside serif style number with a D prefix above the arrow. D6302/18/22/5/8/32/3/4/6/7/9/42/3/54 were the locos involved, depicted here by D6343 at Royal Oak in June 1968 with an up parcels. On the right is another loco of interest, an early blue repainted 08, D4026, later very familiar to me as Toton's 08858 in blue with red coupling rods. (Grahame Wareham)

A motive power shortage in 1970 led to cessation of withdrawals of the hydraulic fleet and a few more Class 22s being put through works: 6308/19/26/30/8/48/52/6. The style differed in so far as there was no longer a need for a D prefix and the lettering switched to the Rail Alphabet style, also swapping position with the arrow. None of the other blue locos received this new style. 6319 was released to traffic in shiny blue in 1971 and almost immediately withdrawn and scrapped by mistake as a preservation bid was being mounted. 6330's career is already over as it stands dumped at Swindon in May 1972 (Grahame Wareham)

Class 33

D6516 in as-delivered condition minus any panel at Basingstoke in September 1966, with an early blue variant seen on the 4TC and 4REP sets, small yellow panels and plain blue livery. Eventually these would appear in Blue/Grey with FYE. Oddly, many Class 33s ran minus the panels as late as 1968 despite these supposedly being compulsory from February 1962. The coaches in the background are green, as was most SR allocated stock. The last green coaches were a few BR mark 1s in the summer of 1970 but, despite their livery, they were seen as far away as Scotland.

D6516 probably bypassed the yellow panels or GFYE stage and emerged from Eastleigh in shiny Rail Blue in May 1967. Most of the numerous late survivors without yellow of any kind did the same, as with Class 20s D8029/30/3. (Grahame Wareham)

Yellow panels were added to many of the Class 33s but, as mentioned earlier, many were plain green as late as 1968, by which time some were in full Rail Blue, others in GFYE and GSP.

D6563 rolls though Plumstead on 8 May 1969 displaying the GFYE style worn by D6501/3/6/10/8/50/3/6/7/59-64/6-8/70-3/5/6/84/8/91/6. D6570 was an oddity in that it had a coaching stock roundel instead of a lion and wheel. The first push/pull-fitted loco, D6580, emerged in green livery with panels but the rest were repainted blue as they were fitted. (Ian Cuthbertson).

Repaints to Rail Blue for the 33s commenced in November 1966 with D6521, which was fitted for push/pull at the same time, and the repaints were complete by May 1971 with D6566 the last to fall. There was little or no variation in the style, as shown here by 33034 at Waterloo on 28 February 1986 with two Waterloo and City tube vehicles in tow. All but two 33s ran in blue, the exceptions were D6502/76 which were accident damage withdrawals in 1964 and 1968 respectively. D6502 is believed to have no panels, while D6576 was GSYP. (Gordon Edgar)

Class 37

Class 37s D6700-31 were delivered in green without yellow panels, but all subsequent locos had them, and the first 32 were quickly retrofitted, as seen here with D6712 at Cambridge on 31 July 1967. By the time of this shot the first few were appearing in Rail Blue. D6937 is believed to be the first repainted around February 1967 with a cabside arrow and a D prefixed number. D6937 lasted under three years in green livery, D6712 rather longer until late 1972. (Bill Wright)

Most green 37s got FYE added from 1967 onwards, the last known GSYP survivor was D6841 in the summer of 1970. This is D6817 at Manchester Piccadilly with the Manchester-Harwich 'Boat Train' on 14 June 1968. The loco has acquired the 'Rail Alphabet' style numbers that came in with the corporate image and as this is still a few weeks before the end of steam and the subsequent dropping of the D, it remains under its original identity of D6817. The stock is already mostly blue/grey liveried, coaching stock went into the new colours far more rapidly than locomotives. (Bill Wright)

Above: Early Class 37 repaints to blue featured cabside arrows and numbers, initially with D prefixes until the style of cabside number and central bodyside arrow became standard from December 1968.

Just pipping the post with a November 1968 repaint to blue, but in time to bypass the D prefix, was 6848 seen here at Grangemouth on 10 June 1972. The locomotives concerned were D6753/73/97, D6823/31/45/89, D6937/45/92 before the D was dropped, and 6812/20/24/35/48/70 after. 6831/45/89 and 6945 lost their D before too long. 6945 and 6992 were renumbered into TOPs with cabside numbers and arrows as 37245 and 37292. (Dave Jolly)

Opposite above: Two oddities were 6882/3 repainted by Crewe Works in March and April 1970 respectively. Those of you who had the Tri-ang model of D6830 will recognize 6882 seen here in September 1973 at Cardiff. When renumbering to 37182 came in 1974 the new number was applied on top of the old and it ran in traffic like this for some time, alongside more traditional 'Early Blue' style 37245/92. Since these two were repainted long after steam was in use, neither had a D prefix, unlike the Tri-Ang model: today's modellers would raise the roof at such an occurrence! (Brian Ireland)

Opposite below: Few Class 37s lasted in green livery long enough to run with a TOPS number: 37009, 37176/86, 37207/10/4/8/25/9-34/9/44/50/65/7/85/9 are the known examples. There may have been one or two more that cannot be substantiated. 37225, shown at Bristol on 19 August 1974, typifies the look of most of them, being in poor external condition and extremely dirty. The old 6925 number has been overpainted in green on the secondman's cabside window.

Oddly 37232/50 retained a double arrow on green. D6921 and 6982 also had them on green courtesy of Doncaster but both went blue before TOPS. The final green liveried 37 was 37244 which lasted until October 1976. (Paul Townsend)

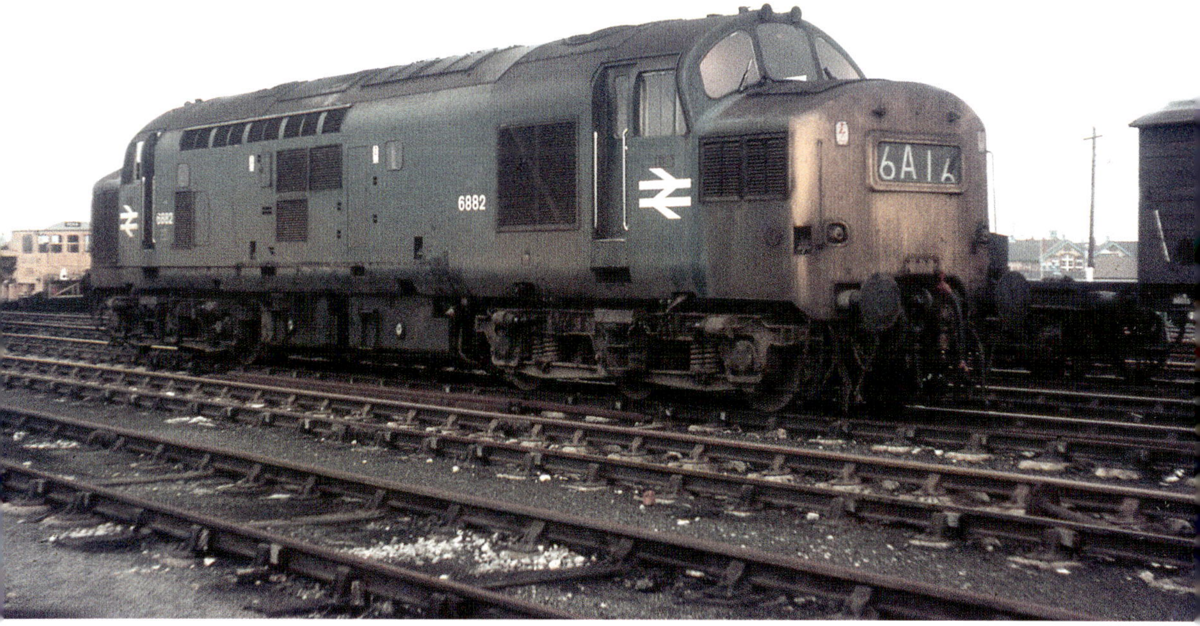
6882

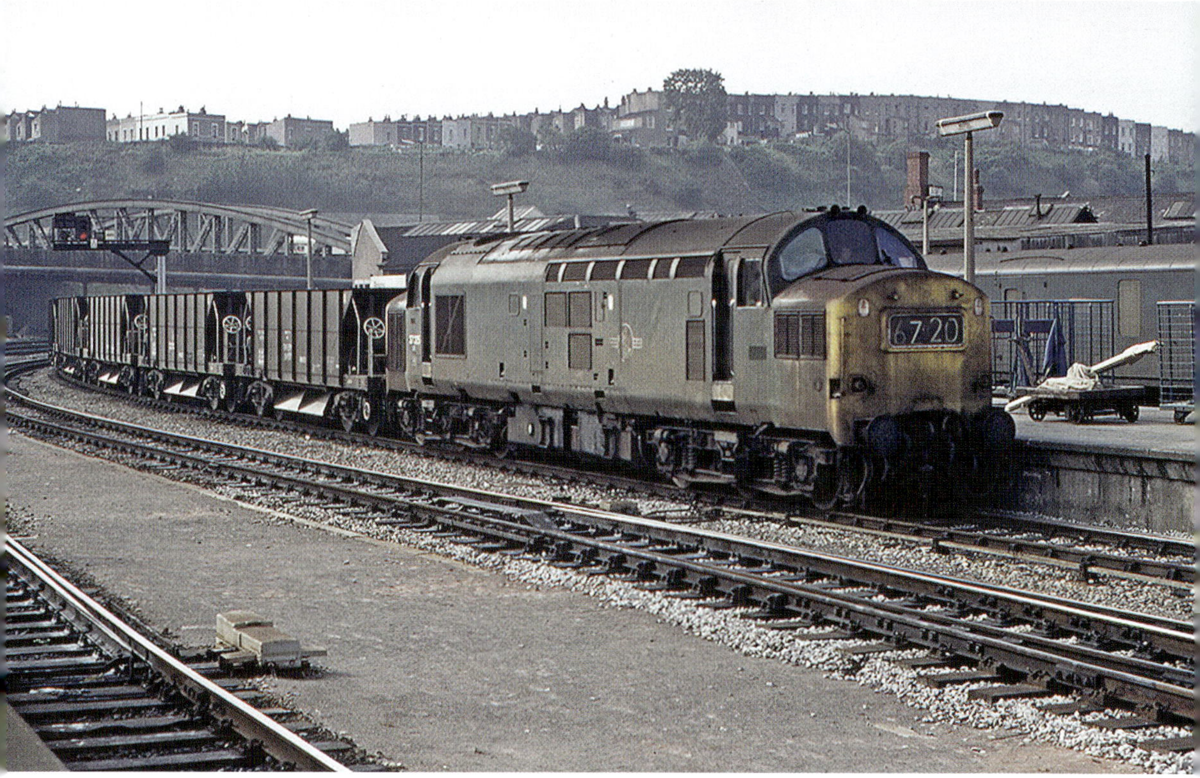

The final Rail Blue version applied to all members of the class (apart from early withdrawal D6983) was a cabside number and a central body arrow. 6836 was probably the first to appear like this, in December 1968. Here in triplicate are 37301/4/8 (formerly D6601/4/8) at Cardiff Central on 15 April 1978 with the famous Port Talbot-Llanwern Iron Ore workings. (David Hayes)

'Hymeks'

The first few Class 35 'Hymeks' were delivered without yellow panels. After D7019 all had yellow panels from new and the rest quickly had them applied.

Green 'Hymeks' were in a most attractive livery, worn by all 101 members of the class. The windows were given white surrounds and the light green solebar band broke up the slab-sided body. Thirteen of the class never wore Rail Blue: D7002/3/5/6/8/13/4/20/1/4/5/54/60. The last in traffic was D7054 until the end of 1972 when it had become quite a celebrity. Here, D7070 trundles through Newport on 2 February 1968 with a mixed freight. (Bill Wright)

A few green 'Hymeks' also ran with GFYE and the yellow extended around the cab windows; D7000/9/13/4/ 6/8/20/3/31/84/92-4/7. Some sources also include D7075 in that list but forty years looking has not produced any photographic proof. Most of the GFYE locos were repainted into Rail Blue with full yellow ends, but D7013/4/20 never were and ended up on the scrap line in that livery alongside the aforementioned GSYP examples. Here, D7094 runs light engine though Cardiff Central in 1968. (Fred Castor)

Above: In common with many other WR hydraulic classes, several 'Hymeks' appeared in blue with small yellow panels, the result of the aforementioned dispute over visibility from PW staff. The first three, D7004/7/51, had blue surrounds to the windows which made for a rather drab appearance, but later examples had the white window surrounds like D7046, seen here at Ranelegh Bridge in March 1968, which hugely improved matters. Engines involved were D7010/2/27/34/6/40/6/7/8/52/6/7/9/64. D7004 of the plain blue trio later had white window surrounds. D7007/10/34/6/40/6/7/51/2/6/7/9 remained in the blue SYP until withdrawal. (Grahame Wareham)

Opposite above: D7033 was the first 'Hymek' into blue in November 1966, predating the SYP examples with a slightly different take on the livery. Although it had full yellow ends, they did not wrap around the front end quite so much as on later repaints and the arrow was sited a little higher up the bodyside. The ones done in BSYP also had the arrow there, and at least D7063 did too, of the first few done when the style reverted to BFYE in 1967. The next few done in late 1966 and early 1967 had small yellow panels before the style changed back to that of D7033.

Opposite below: One of the very last 'Hymeks' to go Rail Blue was D7011 in August 1971, along with D7032 a week or so afterwards. General withdrawals started in September and most of the class went in 1971/72, including all those still in the early blue with panels and those still in green, leaving a few Rail Blue locos to linger on for a few more years until 1975. D7011 displays the final style of Rail Blue applied to most members of the class with the fuller style of yellow ends, here at Reading in May 1974. Most locos retained the raised cabside numerals but many had the D removed or simply painted out in blue, as seen here. Despite a few surviving into 1975, the Hymeks were not included in the 1973 TOPS renumbering scheme and none became 35 001 etc. (Grahame Wareham)

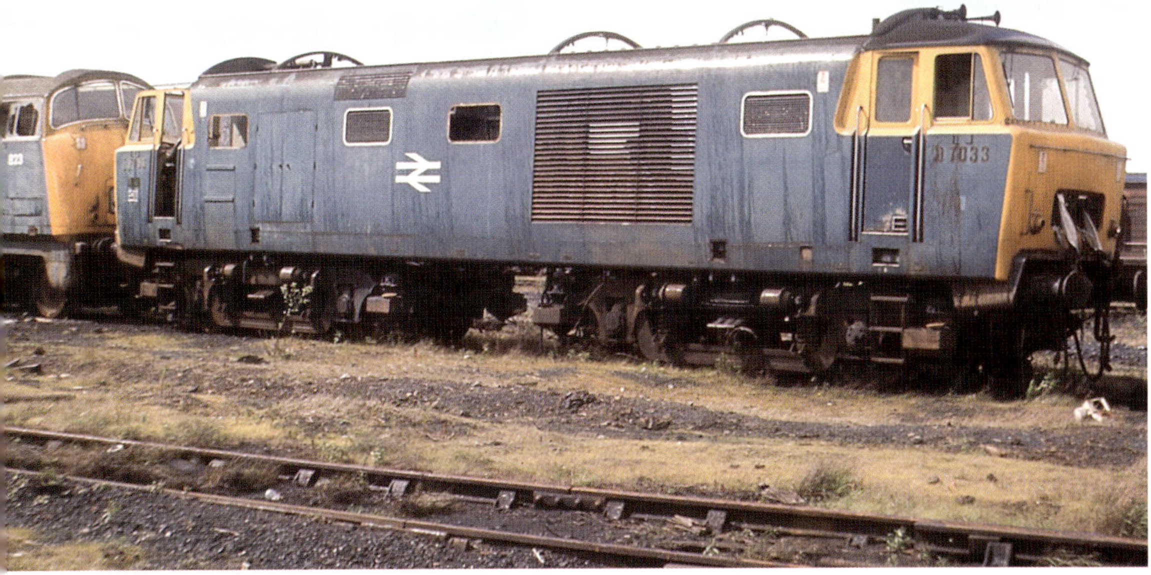
7033

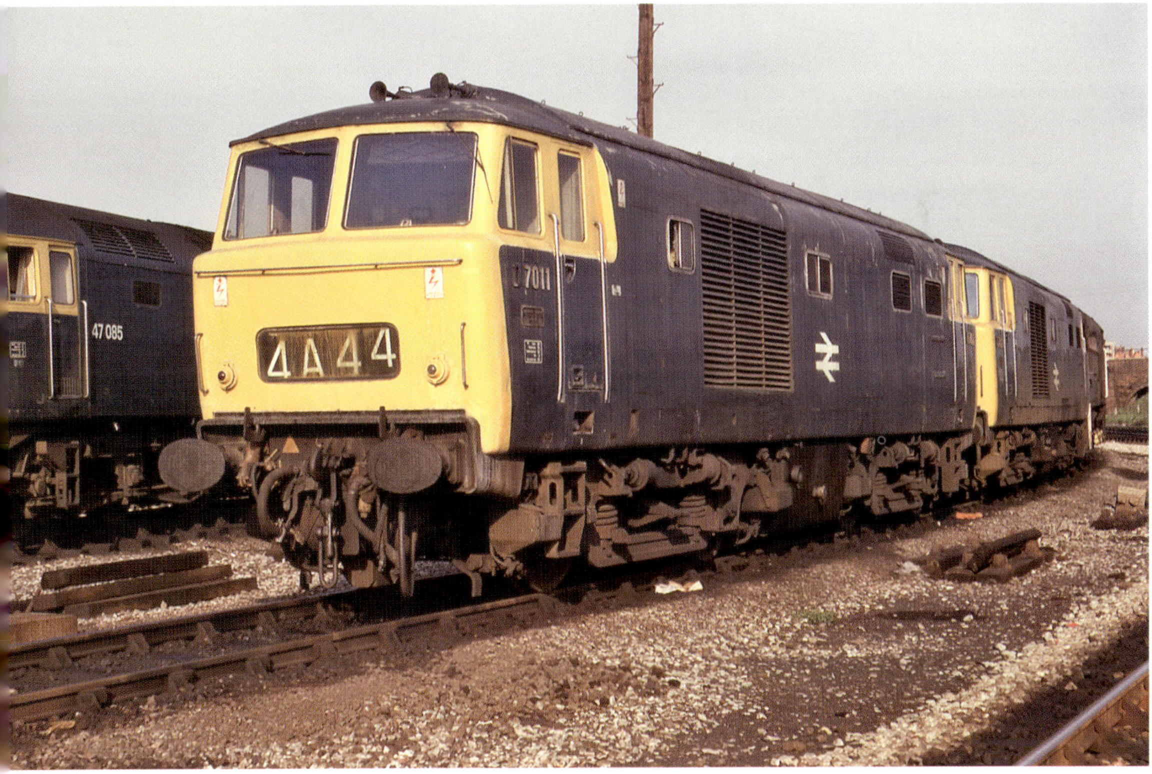
4A44
7011
47 085

Class 20

Above: Class 20s were delivered in two distinct batches, D8000-127 from 1957-62 and then the headcode-fitted D8128-99, and D8300-27 in 1966-8 when it became apparent that other type 1 locos were nothing like as reliable as the steadfast Class 20.

The first batch, D8000-127, were all delivered without panels, at least it is believed so: D8127 was photographed in 1962 without at any rate. The sheer reliability of the type and the odd LMR practice of releasing ex-works locos in green in the 70s ensured large numbers of the class lasted into the TOPS era in green and, in fact, 20141 was the last 'proper' main line Green TOPS engine, not going blue until May 1980.

Green TOPS 20s were 20014-6/8/20-3/5/6/8/45/7/56/7/75, 129-33/7/8/40/1/4-7/9-56/8/62/45/7/9/70/ 4/5/7, 228. 20014 was the only one not to get Rail Blue, being withdrawn in March 1976 still green.

20075 looks very worn at Frodingham on 22 August in the hot dry summer of 1976 and it would get more and more battle weary until finally gaining blue in November 1979. It retains its coaching stock roundel applied to D8050-127 and oddly D8014. (Trevor Hall)

Opposite above: An interesting pairing here: D8071 at Spean Bridge in August 1968 in green with small yellow panels (received after 1962) is fairly typical of the era, but the second loco is one of Inverurie's output with the number in serif and arrow behind the cabside. There were a few like this; D8032/ 72/3/6/99, 8112 and even one, 8034, done in April 1969 minus the D. Both have the recessed cab side for tablet equipment as fitted to D8028-34/70-127. (Topticl.com)

Opposite below: GFYE in triplicate at Stratford on 7 June 1970, with Class 20 D8056 and 47s D1524 and D1563. Very few Class 47s escaped this style, barring the first few repaints to blue, the handful of new build blue engines and the first two withdrawals due to accident damage, D1671 and D1734. The other two early casualties, D1562 and D1908, were amongst the ranks of the two tone GFYE. The two 47s here were not to remain green for long, going blue in January and April 1971 respectively, but D8056 lasted until 1975 as Green TOPS 20056. (Gordon Edgar)

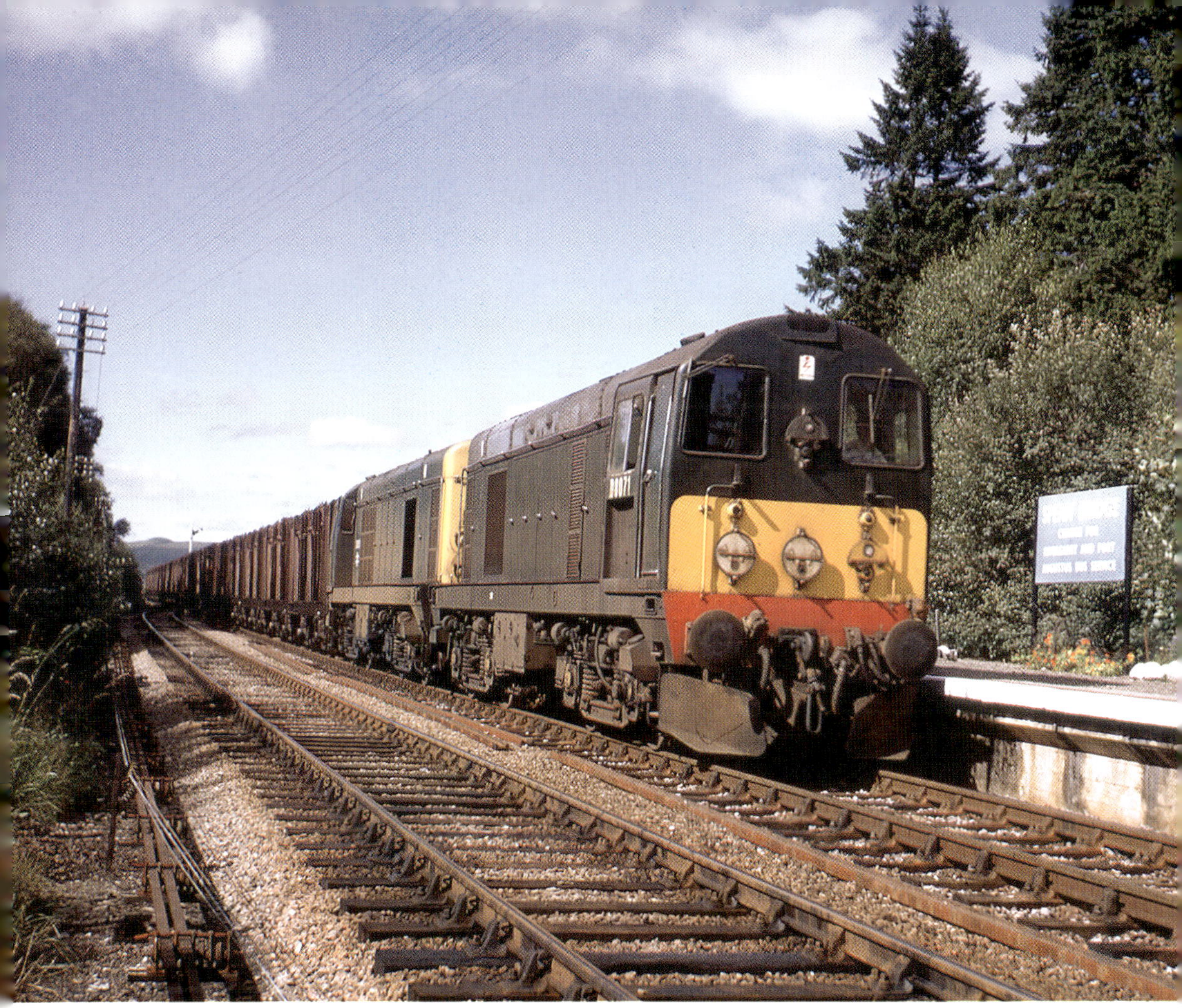

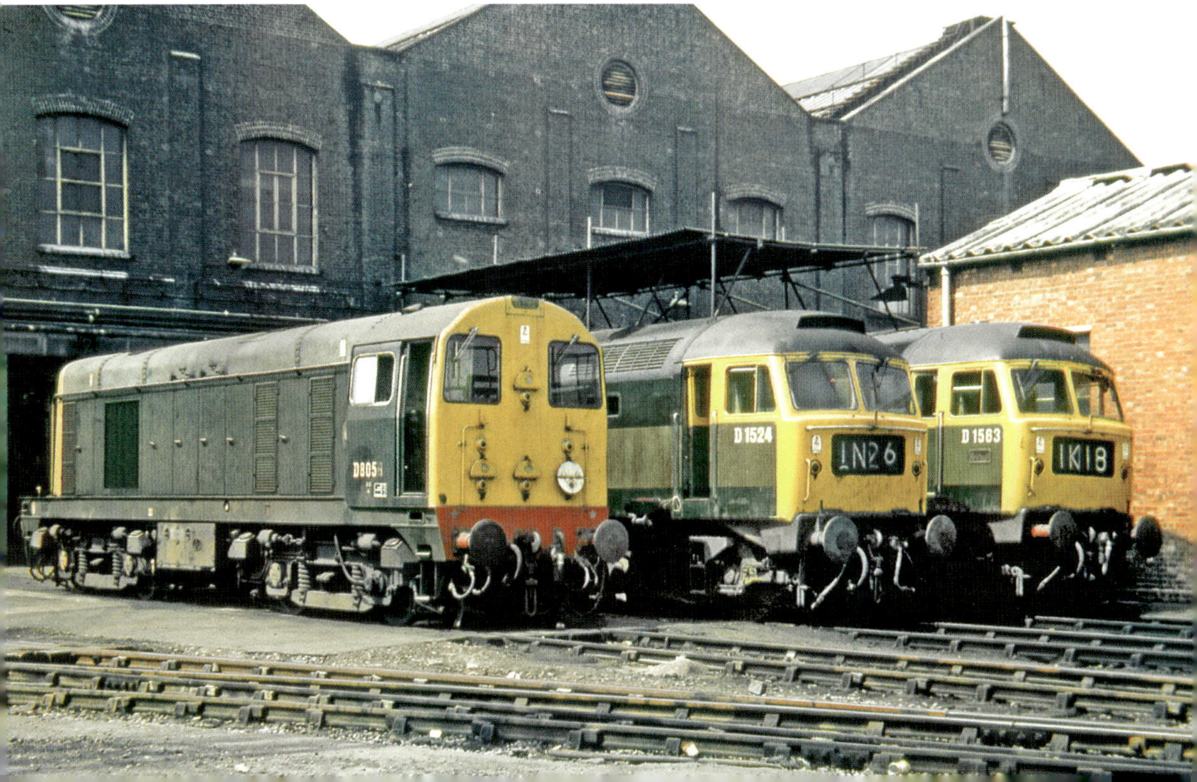
D 1524
1N26
D 1563
1K18

The blue livery on Class 20s varied according to era and which works applied it. New builds from D8178 on had the number above the arrow on the cab, Crewe repaints done early on in 1966/67 followed the same pattern but with serif numbers on the first few, D8001/10/46/8/9. Later repaints from 1968 on were usually the other way around with the number below the arrow on the cab. Glasgow usually placed the arrow on the bodyside and the number on the cab, but occasionally on the body too. Inverurie had, as ever, its own idiosyncrasy, with serif numbers and bodyside arrows, in some cases bodyside numbers too. Here, a vintage June 1970 Crewe job, 20063 rests at Frodingham on 22 August 1976. After 1974 the Glasgow style was gradually adopted and very few lasted to the end in anything else. (Trevor Hall)

Contrasting blue styles with recess fitted 20028 and standard blue 20025 at Frodingham on 23 October 1977. Both of these engines had been in green livery with TOPS numbers not too long beforehand. (David Hills)

Class 15

None of the 44 Class 15 locomotives ever received Rail Blue despite surviving in traffic until 1971, which makes it more puzzling than ever that classes which vanished years before did. The Class 15s were all delivered in all-over green, all had SYP applied and most had FYE later. A mix of both varieties had arrows instead of lion and wheel logos and a mix of numbering styles, serif and Rail Alphabet. A contrast in front-end styles can be seen here; 8229 minus the D and with FYE and arrows stands next to 8230 with SYP at Ipswich on 2 May 1971 a couple of months after withdrawal. (Gordon Edgar)

Another GFYE class 15, this time with serif numbers, D prefix and arrow, D8231 at Ipswich in October 1971. D8202/6/12/23/30/3/41 were scrapped with panels, D8208/32/8 are not recorded as having full yellow ends and I assume they were scrapped with panels but it is not known with certainty. (Stuart Ray)

Four Class 15s survived past 1971 as Carriage heating units; D8203/33/7/43 renumbered as ADB968003/1/2/00 respectively. ADB968001 remained in GSYP with a lion and wheel logo. The other three were GFYE, 968000 with an arrow, 968002 with no logo and 968003 with a lion and wheel. All four were still in use past June 1980 when 08934 went blue, and arguably qualify as the last real green liveried BR locos. ADB968000 was later repainted in an odd shade of apple green, retaining the arrow logo as seen here at Derby Test Centre on 27 April 1982 (Steve Ireland)

Class 16

None of the ten NBL Class 16s lasted long enough to go blue but most got FYE applied. This is surprising because FYE was introduced in February 1967 and the whole class was gone by September 1968, not even lasting long enough to lose their D prefixes.

D8401 is on the scrapline at Cohen's, Kettering in August 1969 next to SYP D8405. D8404 and D8409 also did not have FYE and 8408 is unknown. It did have a very unusual yellow end style at one point, almost in the centre of the nose, but I am unsure if that was there to the end. (Grahame Wareham)

Class 17

The incredibly short-lived Class 17 Claytons, none with a working life longer than nine years, nevertheless managed to gain quite a number of class members with GFYE and a surprising number in Rail Blue.

8536 has lost its D prefix and gained FYE but is already dumped out of use at St Rollox in this 1972 picture. The last members of this class did not enter service until 1965 and withdrawals began in 1968. D8611 managed less than four years in traffic from December 1964 to October 1968. Many, like 8536, gained full yellow ends. Surprisingly 8536, in common with many, lay dumped around Glasgow for years and was not finally scrapped until December 1975. (Grahame Wareham)

D8583, newly ex-works in shiny Rail Blue, is seen here at Haddington in November 1967. This particular engine was to run in traffic until September 1971 but several blue examples were withdrawn as early as 1968. Rail Blue examples were 8500-3/7/10/2/20/2/3/5-7/9/32/4/8/40/2/3/5/50/6/7/64/5/7/70/3/4/7/80/2/3/98, 8606. 8521 was blue but in an unusual all-over style with yellow ends done after its withdrawal. 8512/98 were actually withdrawn in green with FYE and repainted by Derby test centre later on. (TopTicl.com)

Class 55

The 22 Deltics were delivered green minus any panels. All quickly had them applied post-February 1962. Most also received FYE onto their green livery from 1967. D9010, uniquely, ran in GFYE with cabside arrows applied at Doncaster. It is believed that most Deltics, excepting D9002/4/8/16/20/1, had GFYE. There is some doubt over D9019. But this was a short-lived variation as the Deltics were all Rail Blue by the end of 1969. D9006 is seen here at Darlington on 30 April 1968, looking quite anachronistic with a rake of blue/grey stock. (Bill Wright)

Newcastle Central, 8 September 1976, and Deltic 55005 is about to depart with an ECML working. The first Deltic into blue was D9002 in October 1966, just weeks after the last A4 Pacifics were withdrawn further north. As befitting their status as the fastest and most powerful locos in daily use, the Deltics quickly gained a new blue livery, all being done by late 1969. I am quite grateful that my first sight of a Deltic at Newark in late 1968 was a green loco, D9014, the only green one I saw in service. 45069, shown on the left (ex D121), predated the Deltics into blue in February 1969. 55005 was a late survivor in green until August of that year. (David Hayes)

55003 *Meld* at King's Cross, 14 July 1979, shows the increasing amount of personalization that depots were getting away with by then. Such aberrations would have been unthinkable just a year or two before. Finsbury Park applied white window surrounds to its Deltics and also to its Class 31s after Stratford had led the way via silver roofs for its 31s and 47s. York rather dourly painted them back blue when they transferred north to finish their working lives. (Bill Atkinson)

Possibly the only class less successful and shorter-lived than the 'Claytons' were the Class 14s. 56 locomotives were built in 1964/5 and all were withdrawn between December 1967 and April 1969. D9554 was only in service for two years and five months. Quite surprisingly, none were repainted from the livery as built and none, as far as I am aware, even lost the D prefix. Oddly most survived in industrial use for decades and a great number still exist in preservation because of their long survival after the steam era.

D9522, then still nearly new but with only just over two years to go till withdrawal, is Reading station pilot in August 1965. Sadly D9522 was one of the few that was not sold into industrial use and was scrapped before the end of steam in May 1968. (Grahame Wareham)

Class 56

The last new class to have members delivered in Rail Blue was of course the 56s from 1977 onwards. All up to 56083 were delivered in standard Rail Blue, including 56036, the first one to get the large loco livery in 1978, an event that marked the beginning of the end for the classic era of Rail Blue. 56008 typifies the style here at Wigan Spring's Branch, 15 November 1986. (Martin Hilbert)

Class 53

Another interesting locomotive to appear in Rail Blue was the Brush prototype D0280 *Falcon*. Built in 1961 and employing the same engines as the Class 52 Westerns, *Falcon* was soon left behind by advances in technology and doomed to be a one-off. Initially in a lime green livery, BR painted it into two-tone green in the mid-60s complete with small yellow panels. BR bought the locomotive from Brush in 1970, put it through Swindon Works, renumbered it to 0280 then 1200, and it emerged in Rail Blue to became the sole member of Class 53. Allocated to Bath Road, it worked turn and turn-about with Westerns until 1972 when it was sent to South Wales. Despite surviving in traffic until October 1975 it was not included in the TOPS renumbering scheme of May 1973 and sadly not preserved. Here it is at Newport in 1974 on a mixed freight. (Rail Online)

Prototypes and Ex-big 4

Perhaps the most shocking example of a missed opportunity to preserve diesel locos were 10000/1, the LMS mainline protypes. Despite both lasting until 1968 before scrapping, neither survived because they were withdrawn at the time we were preparing to mourn the steam locomotive. Initially in black, both acquired green livery in the 1950s and 10001 even ran long enough in traffic to gain a small yellow panel. Seen here at Willesden, it lasted until March 1966 before languishing at Derby Works for a few years on the scrapline. (Topticl.com)

The Southern Railway designed a class of main line diesels for evaluation against steam but the three engines, 10201-3, did not appear until 1950, 1951 and 1954 respectively. Basically the precursor of the Class 40, they were all withdrawn in December 1963 and languished on the scrap line for years until broken up in 1968. By their withdrawal they were all in green livery and 10203 had acquired small yellow panels. The other pair was plain green to the end. 10201 is seen at Derby Works open day on 26 August 1967. (Pete Wilcox)

Above: All the 'Big Four' companies built diesel shunters to evaluate against steam and many had surprisingly long lives. LNER built 1945 vintage 15003, one of a class of 4 that survived in traffic until August 1967, when it is seen at Derby Works open day on the 26th of that month. None of the four received Rail Blue and were all scrapped in green. (Pete Wilcox)

Opposite above: The LMS standard shunter design became BR Class 11 in the 1968 classification list. Delivered in black from 1945-52, they began to be repainted into green from 1956 and a few even appeared in Rail Blue: 12038/40/3/7-9/52/62/3/9/71/81-4. 12040/7/62 had D prefixes for some unexplained reason and 12108 a double arrow on its green livery. 12049, later blue, was still black in January 1967 and there may have been others.

12039, still with Gill Sans numbers, looks out of its time at Derby in February 1968 in the company of green Class 27 D5400 and an early blue repaint Class 24 D5099. (TOPticl.com)

Opposite below: Another class earmarked for early withdrawal that still had Rail Blue examples was the SR designed (but BR built) Class 12s, a small class of 26 engines delivered from 1949-52 and withdrawn 1968-71. 15211 is seen at Hither Green in the company of GSYP Class 33 D6547 on 28 August 1967. 15211 is in full Rail Blue livery. It is possible 15212 was also blue as it had double arrows but it looks green in most pictures and the jury is out on that one. (C. Bush)

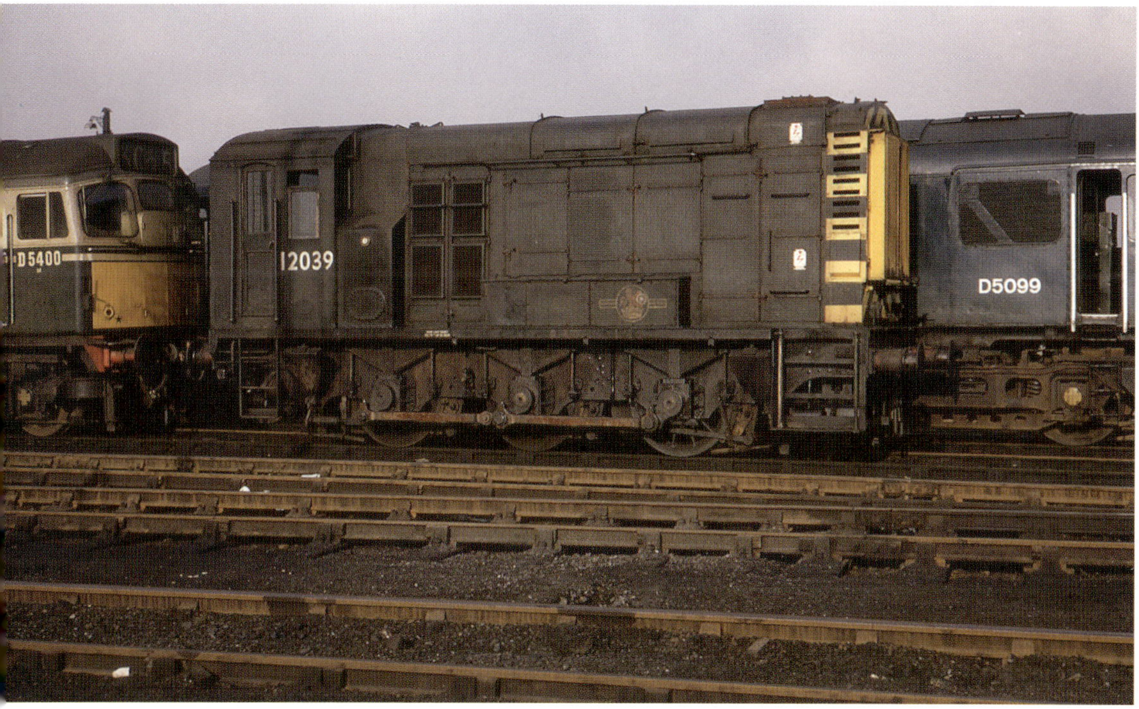
D5400
12039
D5099

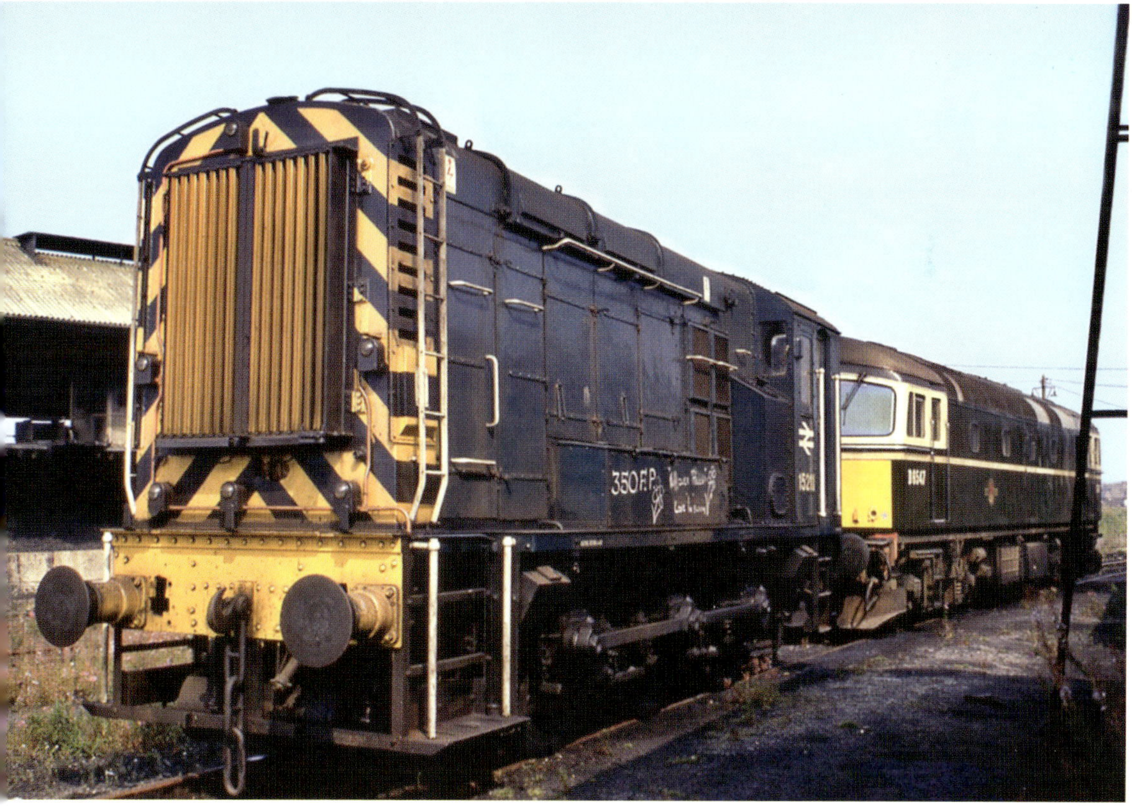
350F.P.

Class 70

The three early electric locomotives of Class 70 numbers 20001-3 survived in service until 1968/9 and each ended up in a different livery. 20001 got a coat of Rail Blue with full yellow ends in May 1967. 20002, seen here at Brighton in 1968, remained in green but with full yellow ends. The third engine, 20003, which had a slightly different body design, was green with yellow panels until withdrawal. 20001 built in 1941 was the oldest locomotive to go Rail Blue although not the oldest piece of rolling stock to do so. (Ron Halestrap collection)

Class 73

The Class 73s were delivered in two batches, E6001-6 in green livery without panels in 1962, and then E6007-49 in 1965-67 in blue livery with yellow panels, as with E6030 seen here in April 1969 at Hither Green. The first few E6007-13 had a grey solebar which greatly added to their appearance. The rest had a more slab-sided look like this example. The six green examples all went to BFYE between 1968 and 1970, with a few running with no panels until late in the 1960s and possibly missing out on them altogether. The later batch all acquired FYE from 1968 onwards. E6030 remained BSYP until at least March 1970 but E6043 lasted until at least October that year. A few were not given any logos at first, E6007-11 for certain, and possibly E6012/3 also. (Grahame Wareham)

All 49 Class 73s, including 1972 accident victim E6027, eventually ran in Rail Blue with full yellow ends by 1970, but the grey roofs were sadly painted over which gave them a boxy look. Here, standard Rail Blue 73111 runs along the coast near Dover with a PW train on 17 February 1980. (David Hills)

Class 73 E6018 ran for a while with strange wraparound full yellow ends and the numbers moved to the bodysides. Here it is at Clapham Junction on 7 September 1967, on a parcels working looking very odd indeed. It was a very early precursor of the large logo style later applied to many classes. It did eventually revert to standard Rail Blue by the summer of 1970. (Pete Wilcox)

Originally a class of 24, the SR Class 71 electrics had ten of the class converted to Electro-Diesel operation and were reclassified as Class 74. The ten rebuilds were painted Rail Blue at the time of the conversion. Originally, the 24 locos were in green minus any panels, but most had panels applied and E5010 had FYE on green. The 14 unconverted locomotives also all appeared in blue and differed little in style to the Class 74s.
71010 stands at Tonbridge on 15 May 1976 in the company of other SR types of Class 33 and 73. (Stuart Ray)

Class 76

Initially the Class 76s, or EM1s as they were known at the time, were delivered in BR black livery as befitting their mixed traffic status, but they began to appear in lined green from the late 1950s and all had yellow panels applied, including slightly different pilot loco 26000 *Tommy*. Many erroneously had E prefixes, something there was no need for as only electric locomotives had 5 figure 2xxxx numbers anyway. It didn't prevent a few 1xxxx diesels getting D prefixes either.
26039 in lined green with panels is seen here at Sheffield Victoria on 23 July 1965. (Bill Wright)

Just one Class 76 appeared in GFYE livery, which is rather surprising as the Class was intact until 1970 with a fair number of green examples extant. To put that into context, by 1970 all but one green Class 47 were GFYE. Electric locos of any kind were remarkable by their absence in any event: just one Class 71 besides this loco is known to have run in the livery. E26031, again wrongly given an E prefix, was the locomotive concerned and it was one of a few never to run in blue, being withdrawn in October 1971. Incidentally, Green Class 76s are usually given away by the lining on the cabside photos if you are using a black and white photo as reference. Here is E26031 resplendent in its unique livery at Barnsley Junction, Penistone on 2 April 1970. (Roger Norton)

Another wrongly prefixed example, E26053, this time in Rail Blue with FYE, seen at Manchester Piccadilly on 13 April 1968. Many early repaints to blue had SYP and lion and wheel logos, and 76022 ran with the lion to the end of its career in 1981.

E26000 *Tommy* was withdrawn in March 1970 in GSYP and a few others withdrawn in 1970/1, 26005/17/31/5/42, never made it to blue livery. Apart from 26031, the others were GSYP. Also withdrawn at the same time were BSYP 26019 and BFYE 26045. (John Ireland)

Class 77

The larger brothers of the Class 76 were the Class 77, the first electric class to disappear from BR after the 1968 classification was introduced. Also initially black, they acquired lined green post-1956, as displayed to fine effect by 27005 *Minerva* at Sheffield Victoria on 23 July 1965. 27000/3 and 27005 were withdrawn in this livery. The locos were sold to Holland in 1968 and ran for many years, with the exception of 27005 which was broken up for spares in 1969. (Bill Wright)

Another Class 77 and another erroneously numbered with an E prefix, E27002 displays the 'Electric Blue' livery at Sheffield Victoria, 21 February 1968. Four of the class received this livery in 1963; 27001/2/4/6. 27004 never received any yellow panels although the other three did. (Bill Wright)

Electrics 81-87

The LMR AC electrics of classes AL1-AL5, later known as classes 81-85, were delivered in 'Electric Blue' a different shade to the monastral blue we know as 'Rail Blue' and minus any yellow panels. Many continued to run well into the '60s without them, as evidenced by Class 81 E3007, seen here at Longsight on 8 August 1965. Most of these engines received yellow panels later on and the attractive crests were replaced by double arrows. Some retained the white roofs even after they were given FYE. Most of Classes 83 and 84 were stored out of use from 1967/8 till 1972 and retained Electric Blue with yellow panels throughout. E3002/9 and E3055, which were withdrawn early due to accidents, remained in the Electric Blue to withdrawal. (Bill Wright)

Above: The contrast between the 'Rail Blue from new' Class 86s and the lighter shade that was applied to the first 100 locos is shown here with E3129 stabled next to a Class 85 at Crewe on 29 May 1966. Although not entering service until 1965, some of these engines did not have yellow panels when new. Some sources suggest E3101-7, E3161-9 were the locos concerned but research has not uncovered any shots other than E3104/63-5 to back that up. (John Evans)

Opposite above: 95 of the 100 locos from the earlier classes made it to TOPS, as here with 82004, the former E3050, seen leaving Crewe on 1 June 1979 with an up passenger working. AC electrics all adopted this style with a cabside number and a central bodyside arrow until the naming of the 86s and 87s, when the arrow moved to the cabside. One exception was 87001 which, after naming, had its number placed halfway down the cabside, making it instantly recognizable from a distance. (Russell Saxton)

Opposite below: A newly named 86, 86103, runs into Nuneaton on 27 August 1981. The arrow has moved to the secondman's cab to allow for the nameplate on the bodyside. The train is formed of Mark 2 stock which was all delivered from 1965 in blue and grey, apart from the first few in maroon, or green if SR allocated. Note the mark 1 coach halfway down the rake, usually the buffet car. (Stuart Ray)

BR: From Green to Blue

The 36 Class 87s were built in 1973/4 and naturally were Rail Blue from the off. Initially they had numbers on all four cabs and a bodyside arrow but were later named and followed the style of the 86s with a cabside arrow. The solitary Class 87/1 87101 had the distinctive silver nameplate *Stephenson* after transfer from 87001 and is seen here on an all blue/grey rake of mark 1 and 2 stock at Crewe on 4 July 1987. (Stuart Ray)

DMUs

The several thousand DMUs delivered from 1954 were all delivered in green livery, initially DMU green (Malachite) and later loco green (Brunswick). Yellow panels were added from 1962, except for the Class 123 which had a curious yellow gangway end cover. The more usual style is shown here on a Cravens Class 105 at Mablethorpe circa 1965. (Jack Ray)

When the Rail Blue style was launched from June 1966 onwards, those warranting the description 'Inter-City' were repainted in blue/grey to match the coaching stock, the lesser units in plain blue. The Class 124s were given the blue/grey treatment from 1966 complete with full yellow ends, as seen here with E51965 at Liverpool Lime Street on 22 May 1979. Initially Class 124 blue repaints had the yellow ends extended around the cab doors; at least E51960/3 were done like this. As far as is known none of the Class 124s appeared in green with full yellow ends, and few DMUs of any kind did. (Martyn Hilbert)

Plain blue Class 100 M56111 stands at Longsight on 19 June 1983, displaying the livery style worn by those DMU classes not designated as 'Inter City'. There was considerable ambiguity over what constituted an 'Inter City' type and what didn't, and examples of the same classes appeared in both liveries in the late '60s. Later on many classes were simply given the blue/grey livery regardless. In common with nearly all DMU classes the Class 100s ran the gamut of green, green with panels, blue with panels and finally blue with full yellow ends. (Russell Saxton)

By the 1970s the BR DMU fleet was approaching 20 years in service and many of the sets were in poor internal condition. A programme of refurbishment was embarked on and vehicles so treated were repainted white with a waist level blue stripe. Examples of Classes 101, 108, 110, 111, 114, 115, 116 and 117 were given this. A four-car formation of Class 108 units in the new livery is seen leaving Chester with the 1015 working to Llandudno in the summer of 1979. (Graeme Phillips collection)

EMUs

In the early '60s most EMUs were in green livery (except the Glasgow 'Blue train' Class 303 and the maroon liveried Class 309s). New builds from 1965 such as AM10s (class 310s) appeared in plain blue with SYP and progressively received full yellow ends as time went on. Inter City types were either repainted or delivered in blue/grey livery, with most types receiving the latter from the early 80s. Coaching stock was given blue livery very quickly compared to locomotives and consequently there were large numbers of blue EMUs with SYP and FYE around in the mid-60s with many types due for early withdrawal included.

The largely forgotten Class 505 Manchester-Altrincham 1500v DC units were built as long ago as 1931 and qualify as almost the oldest items of rolling stock to go Rail Blue. Right at the very end of their service at Altrincham on 10 April 1971, with just three weeks to go, M28580M is still in its early 60s guise of GSYP, surrounded by Rail Blue liveried classmates including M28574M and incorrectly numbered M28592, missing the M suffix to denote its LMS origins. (Gordon Edgar)

SR EMUs were green up till 1966 when new delivery sets began to appear in blue, firstly with SYP and then FYE, later of course in Blue and Grey for the Inter City units. A few different types did appear in GFYE as shown here with 4BUF sets in action, this time with the leading set 3123 in GFYE (not a common livery for any EMU, or DMU come to that) and trailing set 3081 in BFYE at Guildford 18 July 1970. The last GFYE SR EMUs ran until 1971. (Gordon Edgar)

The SR 4BUF design dating back to 1938 had a number of Rail Blue members. All blue (with FYE) example 3077 is seen here at Ascot on 5 December 1970, reduced to working its last months out on Waterloo-Guildford stoppers. The unit is in extremely battered condition, befitting the nickname 'Nelsons' bestowed partly because they ran Waterloo-Portsmouth services but also because they have only one 'eye'. (Gordon Edgar)

Above: One of the unique 1200vDC EMUs of Class 504, M77159, is seen here dumped at Bury, still in green livery. The date of 17 September 1978 was long past the time when any EMU or DMU ran on BR in green but there was a good reason for the late survival of this unit. 26 two-car sets were built for the line in 1959 which was far too many for the service by the late '60s and the unique voltage precluded their transfer to other lines. The first 7 sets M65436-42, 77157-63 were stored from the late '60s but not actually withdrawn and remained at Bury for many years before some were sent to Croxley Green for Class 501 spares. 65438/9 and 77157-60 remained in green, the others were a mix of BSYP (65442, 77162/3), blue with the early wraparound yellow ends (65443) and BFYE (65436/7). 65440 and 77161 were scrapped at Horwich in 1971, presumably green although I don't know for sure. (Martyn Hilbert)

Opposite above: The oldest BR rolling stock to go Rail Blue were the ex-LT EMUs sent to the Isle Of Wight in 1967 to replace the last steam locomotives. Built between 1923 and 1931, the 4VEC and 3TIS sets were painted in all-over Rail Blue and full yellow ends. Later on they acquired blue/grey livery and a few even at the eleventh hour the Network SE livery.
   3TIS set 035 stands at Ryde Pier on 18 November 1978 still in all-over blue. (David Hayes)

Opposite below: A pair of Class 205 DEMUs, set 1103 in Rail Blue leading, makes an attractive sight at Salisbury Tunnel Junction on 29 April 1970. Delivered in green without yellow ends, they progressed through green with panels, Rail Blue with small yellow panels and then full yellow ends, eventually gaining blue/grey livery. Several SR EMU and DEMU classes appeared in green with full yellow ends also. (The late Keith Holt)

Above: 4VEP 7842 at Clapham Junction on 26 August 1981 shows the blue/grey livery worn by the 'Inter-City' classed EMUs in the '70s and '80s. The 4REP and 4TC sets were delivered in plain blue with SYP but all were in blue/grey by the end of 1970 except for 4TC number 424 which went blue soon afterwards. (Stuart Ray)

Opposite above: The 'Blue Pullman' sets operated by the LMR and WR were originally in a striking 'Nanking Blue' livery but corporate identity meant adopting the livery of the Pullman coaches, grey body with a blue band. Full yellow ends appeared in 1967 and the sets were given the Pullman livery between then and March 1970. W60091, part of the last set to remain in the old blue, is seen here dumped at Old Oak Common on 25 July 1974, already withdrawn for over a year. (Ray Honke, 'Mr Deltic')

Opposite below: Unlike parcels stock, pre-nationalization designed passenger stock had largely disappeared by the end of the 1960s and little appeared in blue/grey. A handful of LMS, LNER and GWR designed passenger coaches and sleepers all made it to blue/grey but all had gone by the early 70s. Oddly a few ex-LNER Gresley and Thompson buffet cars repainted into blue/grey lasted almost to the end of the decade, the Gresley designs till late 1977 and the two Thompson ones until 1978.

One of ten Gresley buffets to appear blue/grey is marshalled in the Manchester-Harwich 'Boat Train' at Manchester Piccadilly in 1972. (Stuart Ray)

BR: From Green to Blue

A doubly interesting photograph: from 1956, the SR painted its coaching stock green and the WR put some of its stock in the old GWR chocolate and cream liveries. The former long outlasted the latter in service and this shot of BSK W34885 must be one of the last taken of one in service. On 22 April 1968 Class 47, D1932 takes the empty stock of the 0555 Bristol-Sheffield from Sheffield to Nunnery.

The locomotive, still in GSYP, was one of very few to escape full yellow ends on green, being repainted blue a few weeks after this was taken. (Bill Wright)

Further reading from Key Publishing

As Europe's leading transport publisher, we produce a wide range of market-leading railway magazines.

Visit: shop.keypublishing.com for more details